Poets' Meeting

Poets' Meeting

George Herbert, R. S. Thomas,
and the Argument with God

WILLIAM J. McGILL

McFarland & Company, Inc., Publishers
Jefferson, North Carolina, and London

Permission to use poetry and prose from the works of R. S. Thomas was granted for purpose of this edition alone by the copyright holder Kunjana Thomas and her agent Gwydion Thomas. Materials from *Selected Poems, 1946–1968, Counterpoint, Mass for Hard Times,* and *No Truce with the Furies* are reprinted by permission of the Estate of R. S. Thomas and Bloodaxe Books Ltd. A complete list of the works from which the materials come appears at the end of this volume.

The author has made all reasonable attempts to contact holders of copyright for the specified works. Any omission in attribution should be drawn to the author's attention.

LIBRARY OF CONGRESS CATALOGUING-IN-PUBLICATION DATA

McGill, William J.
    Poets' meeting : George Herbert, R. S. Thomas, and the argument with God / William J. McGill.
        p.   cm.
    Includes bibliographical references and index.

    ISBN 0-7864-1693-9 (softcover : 50# alkaline paper) ∞

    1. Herbert, George, 1593–1633 — Criticism and interpretation. 2. Thomas, R. S. (Ronald Stuart), 1913–2000 — Criticism and interpretation.   3. Thomas, R. S. (Ronald Stuart), 1913–2000 — Religion.   4. Christian poetry, English — History and criticism. 5. Herbert, George, 1593–1633 — Religion.   6. Anglican Communion — England — Clergy.   7. Christianity and literature — England.   8. Theology in literature.   9. God in literature. I. Herbert, George, 1593–1633.   II. Thomas, R. S. (Ronald Stuart), 1913–2000.   III. Title.
PR3508.M35   2004
821.009'3823 — dc22   2003021373

British Library cataloguing data are available

Manufactured in the United States of America

Cover image ©2003 clipart.com

McFarland & Company, Inc., Publishers
  Box 611, Jefferson, North Carolina 28640
  www.mcfarlandpub.com

To my wife, Ellen

Contents

Preface

Wordsworth was there, mountain-
                browed, and Shakespeare,
of course; Dunbar also;
Dafydd ap Gwilym, frowned on
                   by the English.

There were Aeschylus, too,
Catullus and the time-quarried
face that had taken
Yeats' eye.
          Dunbar, swearing,
at the thistles in his beard,
opened the discussion.
                The rest
blinked, until Wordsworth,
shining behind his thought's
                   cloud
answered in iambics to set
Aeschylus booming.
            The consonants
clicked as ap Gwilym
countered, a turnstile
too fast for Catullus
to get through.

         Pray silence,
a voice crackled, Shakespeare
will speak now. And the others
desisted, looking amusedly down,

1

> each from his own slope,
> on the foreshortened figure
> in honest kersey
> poaching its dappled language
> without protocol on the plain.
> — R. S. Thomas, "Poets' Meeting"

The meeting imagined by R. S. Thomas is larger than the one I propose, but it speaks to my purpose. In the preface to his *The English Poetic Mind*, Charles Williams remarks, "Criticism has done so much to illuminate the poets, and yet it seems, with a few exceptions, … still not sufficiently to relate the poets to the poets, to explain poetry by poetry" (p. vi). Quite simply what I intend here is to arrange an encounter between two poets, my two favorite poets, George Herbert and R. S. Thomas.

I first encountered George Herbert when I was a college sophomore, introduced by an English professor at Trinity College, Kenneth Walter Cameron, who devoted what many would have thought to be, at least in those days, an inordinate amount of time to the seventeenth century priest and poet. It was not too much time for me. I bought a copy of F. E. Hutchinson's edition of *The Works of George Herbert*, and for years I have used it as an inspiration and a rest. Though an historian by interest and training, the first article I ever published was about Herbert's view of the Eucharist.

My attachment deepened when I read C. S. Lewis's *Surprised by Joy* and encountered his description of Herbert's impact on his own life and thought. An agnostic at the time, Lewis reports that as he began pursuing a degree in English literature he became aware that all the writers who appealed to him most strongly were Christians, while those who were not seemed cold and brittle. "But," he observes, "the most alarming of all was George Herbert. Here was a man who seemed to me to excel all the authors I had ever read in conveying the very quality of life as we actually live it from moment to moment; but the wretched fellow, instead of doing it all directly, insisted on mediating it through what I still would have called 'the Christian mythology'" (p. 214). Echoing Lewis's experience, I began to find that many authors I read or people I met with whom I felt a particular empathy turned out to be devotees of Herbert. There is then an encircling web of connections which keeps Herbert in my mind, both consciously and unconsciously.

By comparison, R. S. Thomas is a latecomer in my life. I recall noting a reference to him in a church periodical, *The Living Church* I believe, in the 1980s. I recall also my casual and fruitless endeavors to find copies of his works in American bookstores. Finally, in 1989 while attending a summer institute at Harvard, I wandered into the Grolier Book Shop in Cambridge and there found a copy of *Poems of R. S. Thomas* (University of Arkansas Press, 1985). On reading that, "The hook was in my mouth." By virtue of trips to England and various Internet sites devoted to used and rare books, I have subsequently acquired copies of all his published collections. As I have read and reread his poetry, what has struck me most is that, though Thomas has a distinctly different and clearly twentieth-century voice, he too describes "the very quality of life as we actually live it from moment to moment."

In the fall of 1997 I spent a month at St. Deiniol's Research Library, Hawarden, North Wales (helped immeasurably by a Bishop Allin Fellowship from the Episcopal Church). During that time I concentrated on reading Herbert and Thomas side by side. From that experience this manuscript has emerged. I set out on my journey with the vague notion that although some people had said Herbert and Thomas were comparable, nobody had really done a thorough comparison — so why didn't I? By the time I reached St. Deiniol's, however, I had begun to conceive my project in a different way entirely.

Prior to my sojourn at St. Deiniol's, my wife and I had toured the south of England. The highlight of that trip was our visit to Salisbury. We spent hour after hour exploring the cathedral, awed both by its beauty and by its seemingly miraculous nature as a feat of engineering. We also visited the tiny church of Bemerton St. Andrew's, which Herbert had served and where he is buried. My journal of the trip indicates that during those days I began to understand that what I wanted to do was not to make an elaborate comparison, but simply to bring these two voices, Herbert and Thomas, together, to see what they had to say to one another, what manner of conversation might exist between them — and with God.

Serendipitously, included in the ancillary reading I did at St. Deiniol's was the Charles Williams book quoted above. I would note that R. S. Thomas himself adopted a similar strategy in editing *The Penguin Book of Religious Verse*. He eschewed a chronological ordering of the poems in favor of a topical one because he — and the publisher — "felt that chronological sequence can militate against effective juxtaposition of different authors or passages" (p. 7). Williams also observes: "Religious poetry is poetry, not religion. But good poetry does something more than allude to its subject; it is related to it, and it relates us to it" (p. 3). In these observations Williams sets the framework for what I have attempted to do: to let the poets speak to one another and to us on the subjects that most mattered to them.

Parts of this work have already appeared in print in various forms: the discussion of the idea of calling in *The Anglican Theological Review* (82.2, April 2000), the Thomas portions of the chapter on the Incarnation in *Theology Today* (57.1, April 2000), the segment on the poets' flower poems in *Topic: A Journal of the Liberal Arts* (#50, July 2000), a briefer version of the chapter on the Good Friday poems in *The Sewanee Theological Review* (44.3, Pentecost 2001), and the discussion of Thomas's poems entitled "Waiting" in *The Living Church* (February 22, 1998). I wish to thank the editors of those journals for their reception of my efforts.

Needless to say I also thank the trustees of the Bishop Allin Fellowship Fund and the staff of St. Deiniol's Research Library. My debt to St. Deiniol's increased in August 2000, when I spent eight days there attending a course on the spirituality of George Herbert. By that time I had completed the first draft of this manuscript. The opportunity to again use that library was invaluable — as were the ideas and suggestions of Diogenes Allen, professor of philosophy at Princeton Theological Seminary, who conducted the course.

I need also to express special thanks to John McEllhenney, whose own appreciation for and knowledge and understanding of R. S. Thomas has both expanded and confirmed my own readings. Special thanks as well to Gwydion Thomas, R. S. Thomas's son, who cut the Gordian knot that had delayed the process of obtaining permission to use the quotations from his father's works.

Finally, I thank my wife, Ellen, who supported and encouraged me to take the physical journeys to England and Wales as well as the intellectual and spiritual journeys into the heart of the poetry itself of which this work is the fruit.

Introduction

George Herbert (1593–1633) and Ronald Stuart Thomas (1913–2000) are among the truly great English language poets of their respective centuries; certainly they are among the great religious poets in the Christian tradition. That alone brings them into the same household, but the lines that connect these two strikingly dissimilar writers are more complex.

There are obvious similarities between them, the most basic one being that both were priests in the Anglican church and poets for whom religious questions were the primary matter of their art. One may observe other things about them: for both the Cross was a central image — perhaps *the* central image — and the idea of *Deus absconditus* a recurrent theme; both served their pastorates in rural settings and, though for different reasons, that was a conscious choice. They shared a love of nature and music. Both were pacifists. Each employed space as well as text to create meaning, underscoring the sense that language was inadequate to express the fullness of the truth they sought to understand. There is also the fact that Thomas edited a selection of Herbert's verse, with an introduction that provides ample substance for conversation.

Contrarily there are telling differences, none more critical than the historical contexts in which they lived and moved and had their being. Separating them were the Scientific Revolution, the Enlightenment, industrialization, colonialism and post-colonialism, quantum physics, and one could go on — worlds of difference. The seemingly infinite distance, intellectually and culturally, between Herbert's and Thomas's worlds necessarily produced distinctions of perspective, sensitivity, tone, and language.

In the course of the essays that compose this book, the weight of these differences, and of the similarities, will become evident, but they are not the subject. Nor am I attempting a point-by-point comparison and contrast between the two poets. While I have read widely and, I hope thought-fully, in the secondary literature about Herbert and Thomas, and will make occasional references to some of that literature, this is not an academic monograph intended to evaluate the state of scholarship. It is quite sim-ply an effort to bring the two poets into conversation and in Williams's words "to relate the poets to the poets, to explain poetry by poetry." I hope thereby to encourage a greater appreciation and understanding of the two poets and of the great questions with which their poetry deals—and to stimulate the readers to their own conversations with Herbert and Thomas.

2.

George Herbert was born on April 3, 1593, in Montgomery, the sev-enth of the ten children of Richard and Magdalene Newport Herbert. Both parents were from noble families of the English/Welsh border counties and perhaps, therefore, of mixed Anglo-Norman and Welsh extraction. Richard Herbert died in October 1596. Magdalene soon moved with her children to her family home and then in 1599 to Oxford, where her eldest son Edward (later Lord Herbert of Cherbury) was studying. In 1601 she moved to London.

A bright, articulate woman, Magdalene provided her growing chil-dren both a pious and an intellectually stimulating environment. Among the guests at her house were such men as William Byrd, Lancelot Andrewes and John Donne. (On Magdalene's death in 1627 Donne preached a memo-rial sermon.) In 1609 she married Sir John Danvers. A younger man, he nonetheless became a kind and generous stepfather to those children still at home. By that time George had finished his schooling at Westminster School and was preparing to attend Trinity College, Cambridge.

Herbert would remain in Cambridge as student, fellow, lector, deputy to the University Orator and then Orator until at least 1624. In that year he served in Parliament and at its end was most probably ordained to the diaconate. In 1626 he was named canon of Lincoln Cathedral and prebendary of Leighton Bromswold church, although, while he held the living, he was not often in residence. The next several years appear to be a period during which his health suffered much; it may also be the time when he wrote a significant portion of the poems in *The Temple*. In 1629 he married Jane Danvers, a cousin of his stepfather. In 1630 he received the livings of the churches at Fuggleston and Bemerton, just outside Sal-isbury, and was ordained priest at Salisbury Cathedral on September 19 of that year. He would die in Bemerton on March 1, 1633, and was buried there in St. Andrew's Church.

Herbert published none of his English poems during his lifetime. In his *The Life of Mr. George Herbert*, Izaak Walton says that shortly before his death he gave a manuscript of *The Temple* to Edmund Duncon with instructions to deliver it to his friend Nicholas Ferrar at Little Gidding to do with it as he wished. According to Walton, Herbert described the poems as "A picture of the many spiritual conflicts that have passed betwixt God and my Soul, before I could subject mine to the will of Jesus my Master, in whose service I have now found perfect freedom" (John Tobin, ed., *George Herbert. The Complete English Poems*, pp. 310–311). Some scholars have cast doubt

George Herbert from the 1674 edition of his poems.

on whether Herbert actually described his poems in that way. To be sure, Walton is not the most reliable of sources, but if Herbert did not so describe *The Temple*, it yet remains an apt description of the book's effect and is consistent with the preface Ferrar himself wrote for the first edition. That manuscript is not extant, but was the basis for the transcription done at Little Gidding from which the first published edition was printed in 1633. This transcription is in the Bodleian Library at Oxford and is referred to as the B manuscript.

A second manuscript (Williams or W) also exists. In W there are six poems that do not appear in B, but it contains only 69 of the 164 poems in B and also is missing parts of two poems. Of those sixty-nine, twenty-four are substantially different in the two manuscripts, and the ordering is also different. The authoritative modern edition is that by F. E. Hutchinson, *The Works of George Herbert*, Oxford, 1941, which is essentially based on the B manuscript. Hutchinson comments on the two versions on pp. l–lvi of his introduction. (See also, Amy Charles, "The Williams Manuscript and *The Temple*," *Renaissance Papers, 1971*, The Southeastern Renaissance Conference, and her *A Life of George Herbert* [Ithaca, 1977], pp. 181–186.)

I make a point of referring to the issue of the manuscripts here in order to set the foundation for the way in which I approach Herbert's poetry. As noted, Herbert probably had written most of the poems in *The Temple*, at least in first draft, before going to Bemerton. What he did there was to revise a number of the poems and, most importantly, to work out the sequencing of the poems. We cannot accurately and definitively determine the chronological order in which he wrote them and, in any case, I think that question is incidental, if not irrelevant. What matters, what gives *The Temple* its overall effect, is Herbert's intent to present "a picture of the many spiritual Conflicts," not as a strict chronological record of his own life, but as a description of the journey of a pilgrim soul.

This relates to an important aspect of Herbert's poetry, the matter of voice. One book which I have read with particular enjoyment and benefit is James Boyd White, *"This Book of Starres." Learning to Read George Herbert* (Ann Arbor, 1994). White concludes his preface thusly:

> The speakers of Herbert's poems, while in a sense all of course aspects of the author, are not, I believe, mouthpieces for a central and secure self whose utterances can be quoted as representing what Herbert believed. It is in fact the peculiar genius of this poetry to throw every single utterance, without exception, into question, as it is poised in sequence with others or set against them, and in the process to render uncertain as well the identity and stability of the speaking person. This verse, more than any I know, makes simultaneously problematic both the self and its language. For Herbert, truth lies not in what is or can be said at any one moment, but in the relations that can be established among various things that can be said at different times—among the statements, gestures, and voices that make up his verse. The meaning of his poetry accordingly lies not in particular utterances but in its iridescent movements from point to point [pp. xxi-xxii].

In many respects I agree with this argument and I have responded to White's "reading" of Herbert because I had reached similar conclusions about *The Temple* long before I had read his book. But I would add this: while "The speakers ... are not ... mouthpieces for a central and secure self," they are distinctly and specifically, not just "in a sense ... aspects of the author." The speakers are indeed several selves, but each is Herbert.

> Oh, what a thing is man! how farre from power,
>   From settled peace and rest!
> He is some sev'rall men at least
>   Each sev'rall houre.
>   — Giddinesse

The individual poems were written out of Herbert's own experience and we may take them to represent the variations and vicissitudes of his spiritual life. However, the presentation of them, the final sequencing of the manuscript, does not constitute a spiritual autobiography. Rather it is an effort to give shape to the character of the Christian pilgrimage, to "the very quality of life as we actually live it from moment to moment."

3.

Ronald Stuart Thomas was born on March 29, 1913, in Cardiff, the son of T. H. and Margaret Thomas. For a time during the First World War the family lived in Liverpool, his father being an officer in the merchant navy. When he was five they moved to Holyhead, Anglesey, a more convenient location for his father. Eventually Thomas attended University College, Bangor, and then St. Michael's Theological College in Llandaff. Ordained in 1937, he served curacies in Chirk (1936–1940) and Hanmer (1940–1942), where he was also priest-in-charge of the church in Talarn Green, then had churches of his own in Manafon (1942–1953), Eglwys-fach (1953–1967), and finally Aberdaron (1967–1978). In 1940 he married the painter Mildred (Elsi) Eldridge. They had one son, Gwydion. Following his retirement from the parish ministry they continued to live on the Llyn peninsula at Sarn y Rhiw. After his wife died in 1991 he remained there until remarrying and moving in 1994 to just outside Holyhead. Subsequently, however, he returned to the Porthmadog area, where he died on September 26, 2000.

He had begun to compose poetry in Bangor and published individual poems during his early years in the priesthood, writing in English because that was his native language — he called it his "mother's milk" language. He would not begin to learn Welsh until he was in his thirties and while subsequently he would write and publish prose in Welsh, he never felt comfortable composing poetry in what was for him a second language. His first collection, *Stones of the Field*, appeared in 1946. His first significant recognition came in 1955 when he published *Song at the Year's Turning*, which included new poems as well as selections from his earlier collections. In the introduction to that volume the poet John Betjeman wrote:

> This retiring poet had no wish for an introduction to be written to his poems, but his publisher believed that a "name" was needed to help sell the book. The "name" which has the honour to introduce this fine poet to a wider public will be forgotten long before that of R. S. Thomas [p. 14].

In the same year he received the Heineman award. From that point on each new collection (more than twenty) received widespread notice. In 1997 he was nominated for the Nobel Prize in Literature.

The original take on him — and one that has clung to him in the minds of some — was that he was a rural poet. From the publication of *Not That He Brought Flowers* (1967), however, he began to be thought of as a religious poet, though at times he published collections that reflected his ardent Welsh nationalism. A recent tourist guide (*The Rough Guide to Wales)* sees that as his most characteristic feature and the obituary in the *New York Times* was headed "Welsh Nationalist R. S. Thomas Dies." But any such qualifiers fail utterly to do justice to the scope of his enterprise and his literary stature. Necessarily, over such a long and productive career, he ranged broadly in his subject matter. Finally, however, at the heart of his dual vocation as poet and priest, one finds dynamic tensions between belonging and not belonging, between Welshness and Englishness, between belief and uncertainty. The creative force of these tensions again and again finds expression in his poetry — in the words chosen, the phrasings crafted, the imagery discovered. He had many voices: poet, priest, Welsh nationalist, dweller in the country, pacifist, autodidact widely read in modern philosophy and science, all these things— and more.

Personally, he had the reputation of being a recluse, a reputation primarily generated by his standoffishness toward the English. Those who knew him, however, found him engaging. To be sure, he was a private, even a shy, man and he resisted the idea that his poetry was highly personal and autobiographical. Yet poets write from experience and observation and they write about things and themes that are important to them. Thomas certainly did. If we cannot say that the bulk of his work is autobiographical, we nonetheless can say it gives voice to a discerning and sensitive observer of the world whose poetry, to invoke the words of Lewis about Herbert, describes "the very quality of life as we actually live it from moment to moment." And we can say of him, as White said of Herbert, that "The meaning of his poetry accordingly lies not in particular utterances but in its iridescent movements from point to point."

4.

I begin with an essay dealing with Herbert's and Thomas's sense of calling as priests and poets because all else follows from that. I then attempt to engage them on a series of topics which relate most particularly to their roles as parish priests: ministry, the Bible, the Eucharist, and corporate and personal prayer. There follow several essays dealing with broader questions of the human condition: faith, sin, love, reason and science, and nature. I conclude by considering their poems about Christmas, Good Friday and Easter.

This structure is not serendipitous, but neither is it strictly linear. The sense of it arises from the nature of the poets' own enterprise and, I hope, becomes evident in the reading. In any event, I have tried to engage them in conversations, to see what they have to say to one another, and how the work of one might enhance our understanding of the other. Finally, the "truth

R.S. Thomas, Anglesey, ca. 1997 (courtesy Gwydion Thomas).

[of my argument] lies not in what is or can be said at any one moment, but in the relations that can be established among various things that can be said at different times—among the statements, gestures, and voices that make up ... [their] verse" (White, p. xxii).

I

The Calling: The Vocations of Priest and Poet

The obvious place to begin is with the idea of calling, as priest and as poet. Whatever may divide and distinguish Herbert and Thomas from one another, they share these common vocations. Of course, there have been other poets who have been priests and other priests who have been poets. Indeed, in the Anglican communion which both served as priests the dual vocation seems almost commonplace. In *The Poetic Imagination. An Anglican Spiritual Tradition* (London, 1999), L. William Countryman has argued that lyric poetry has played a distinctive role in the development and articulation of Anglican spirituality. More particularly, he suggested that the tradition begins in the seventeenth century, the work of such priest/poets as John Donne, Henry Vaughan, and, of course, George Herbert. Since the eighteenth century, the more eloquent bearers of the tradition have been laity, including Thomas Gray, William Blake, Samuel Taylor Coleridge, Christina Rossetti, and T. S. Eliot, but R. S. Thomas stood well within it and his life and career reminds us of the affinity between the two vocations.

Countryman stresses as the elements of the Anglican poetic tradition "a high (but distinctive) regard for scripture, a sense of the spiritual value of nature, an investment in the life of the church, and a sense of the accessibility of the Holy in and through the ordinary and childlike" (p. 37). The "distinctive" quality of the regard for scripture is that Anglicanism has largely mediated the scriptures through its liturgy as part of the common prayer of the church. As A. M. Allchin has remarked, the "relationship between literature and faith implicit in the liturgy becomes explicit in the tradition of Anglican poetry and prose; in the series of distinctly theological poets from John Donne ... to ... R. S. Thomas in our own day" ("Anglican Spirituality," in Stephen Sykes and John Booty, eds., *The Study of Anglicanism*, London, 1988, p. 315).

As priests and poets then, Herbert and Thomas stand within a rich tradition. Of course, it is possible to be both, while having the pursuits to be disjoined or one to be subordinated to the other. There is a less edifying tradition of clerical versifiers who merely dabble in one or both of the vocations. Herbert and Thomas, however, are no ordinary poets, nor were they perfunctory priests. For both the two callings were integrally related and thus indivisible — and that accounts in substantial measure for the quality and character of their verse.

1.

The essence of Herbert's "spiritual Conflict" in regard to his calling to the priesthood is nowhere more finely drawn than in his poem "The Collar":

I Struck the board, and cry'd, No more.
                    I will abroad.
          What? shall I ever sigh and pine?
My lines and life are free; free as the rode,
          Loose as the winde, as large as store.
               Shall I be still in suit?
Have I no harvest but a thorn
To let me bloud, and not restore
What I have lost with cordiall fruit?
                         Sure there was wine
Before my sighs did drie it: there was corn
          Before my tears did drown it.
          Is the yeare onely lost to me?
          Have I no bayes to crown it?
No flowers, no garlands gay? all blasted?
                    All wasted?
Not so, my heart: but there is fruit,
                    And thou hast hands.
          Recover all thy sigh-blown age
On double pleasures: leave thy cold dispute
Of what is fit, and not. Forsake thy cage,
                    Thy rope of sands,
Which pettie thoughts have made, and made to thee
          Good cable, to enforce and draw,
                    And be thy law,
While thou didst wink and wouldst not see.

> Away; take heed:
> I will abroad.
> Call in thy deaths head there: tie up thy fears.
> He that forbears
> To suit and serve his need,
> Deserves his load.
> But as I rav'd and grew more fierce and wilde
> At every word,
> Me thoughts I heard one calling, *Child!*
> And I reply'd, *My Lord.*

"The Collar" epitomizes his story. It speaks of his own desires, his restlessness, his ungratefulness. It speaks also of what he saw as God's great mercy.

Both at Westminster School and then Trinity College, Cambridge, Herbert distinguished himself as a scholar and, having completed his baccalaureate, he was chosen as a fellow of Trinity College. He began to teach as well as to pursue the masters, then the normal route to ordination. At that time (1618), he wrote his stepfather, Sir John Danvers:

> ... I want Books extremely; You know Sir, how I am now setting foot into Divinitie, to lay the platform of my future life, and shall I then be fain alwayes to borrow Books, and build on anothers foundation? What Trades-man is there who will set up without his Tools? Pardon my boldness Sir, it is a most serious Case, nor can I write coldly in that, wherein consisteth the making good of my former education, of obeying that Spirit which hath guided me hitherto, and of achieving my (I dare say) holy ends [*Works*, p. 364].

Thus ordination clearly seemed his goal.

But, as he later wrote in *A Priest to the Temple*, "Of Pastors ... some live in the Universities, some in Noble houses, some in Parishes residing on their cures" (*Works*, pp. 225–226). His social status and his academic success led him to think more of the first two paths than the last. That inclination received encouragement when he was chosen first a Reader in Rhetoric (1618), and then Deputy Public Orator of the University. In 1620 he was chosen Public Orator. As he explained to his stepfather,

> The Orators place (that you may understand what it is) is the finest place in the University, though not the gainfullest; ... but the commodiousness is beyond the Revenue; for the Orator writes all the University Letters, makes all the Orations, be it to King, Prince, or whatever comes to the University; to requite these pains, he takes place next the Doctors, is at all their Assemblies and Meet-

ings, and sits above the Proctors, is Regent or Non-regent at his pleasure, and such like Gaynesses, which will please a young man well [*Works*, pp. 369–370].

The prospect of employment at the court was not beyond his thinking though he would deny it. He reported that Sir Francis Nethersol, whom his stepfather had approached on his behalf, feared "this place being civil … [might] draw me too much from Divinity … but I … wrote him back, that this dignity, hath no such earthiness in it, but it may very well be joined with Heaven; or if it had to others, yet to me it should not" (*Works*, p. 370). It may have been of such rationalizations that he was thinking later when he wrote:

> Lord, with what care hast thou begirt us round!
>   Parents first season us: then schoolmasters
>   Deliver us to laws; they send us bound
> To rules of reason, holy messengers,
> Pulpits and Sundayes, sorrow dogging sinne,
>   Afflictions sorted, anguish of all sizes,
>   Fine nets and strategems to catch us in,
> Bibles laid open, millions of surprises,
> Blessings beforehand, tyes of gratefulnesse,
>   The sound of glorie ringing in our eares:
>   Without, our shame; within, our consciences;
> Angels and grace, eternall hopes and fears.
>   Yet all these fences and their whole aray
>   One cunning bosome-sinne blows quite away.
>   —"Sinne (I)"

The attractions of the civil life were great and his hopes were perhaps not inconsiderable. His family connections afforded him opportunity, including service in Parliament (1623–24) and his academic successes drew notice. As Orator his work drew the attention of noteworthy patrons, among them the Duke of Richmond, the Marquis of Hamilton, and King James himself. No less important, however, to this seeming equivocation about his pursuit of ordination was a negative force that restrained him: his own sense of unworthiness, a real and recurrent element in his life. As Nicholas Ferrar noted in his preface to *The Temple*, Herbert claimed as his own motto the words of Jacob in Genesis 32:9–10, "Lesse than the least of Gods mercies." That sense found clear expression in his later poetry as he pondered the priestly vocation:

Blest Order, which in power dost so excell,
That with th'one hand thou liftest to the sky,
And with the other throwest down to hell
In thy just censures; fain would I draw nigh,
Fain put thee on, exchanging my lay-sword
      For that of th'holy Word.

But thou art fire, sacred and hallow'd fire;
And I but earth and clay: should I presume
To wear thy habit, the severe attire
My slender compositions might consume.
I am both foul and brittle; much unfit
      To deal in holy Writ.
        —"The Priesthood," ll.1–12

Izaak Walton makes much of the deaths in 1624–1625 of each of his great patrons as the precipitating events that turned him back to thoughts of a clerical vocation. Without rehearsing the specifics of academic and ecclesiastical regulations, Herbert in 1623–1624 had reached the point when he had to make a decision about ordination to the diaconate. If he had seriously considered a civil career his experiences in Parliament may have proven to him that his temperament was not suited to it.

In his still admirable *George Herbert. His Religion and Art* (Cambridge, Mass., 1954, pp. 40–42), Joseph Summers pointed out a particular issue that separated Herbert from the direction of English politics in 1623. This was the time of the failed negotiations for a marriage alliance between England and Spain (conducted in the context of the religious tensions created by the Thirty Years War in Europe). Prince Charles returned from those negotiations eager for war against the Spanish. In October Herbert gave an oration celebrating Charles's safe return. While it contained the typical laudatory remarks of such a piece of public rhetoric, it also made clear that Herbert stood with James's opposition to making war. Having made such a declaration publicly, Herbert may have understood that a court career was unlikely. One might argue, however, that he felt free to speak because he had no such hopes, or had already abandoned them.

Doubtless, also, his mother and her great friend, John Donne, encouraged him toward ministry and he was ordained, most probably in November, 1624, before the deaths of Hamilton and James I. Again, if we may credit the attitudes evident in his poetry, the inhibiting force was always more his own sense of unworthiness, than it was any avidity for "the ways of honor and pleasure." Even yet, his own disposition and his frail health (another recurrent theme in his life) inclined him to believe that he could best exercise his ministry through his scholarship.

The Bishop of Lincoln granted him a cathedral canonry and the living of Leighton Bromswold. These assignments were an easy yoke in terms of duties, affording him the chance to serve in a manner he felt consistent with his powers. In retrospect, he would come to see this somewhat grudging assent to vocation as evidence of too much pride: he would serve God, but he would tell God how to use him. For the moment, however, he wrapped that pride in a false humility, proclaiming his unworthiness to assume fully the dignity and the duty of priesthood.

Ill health and sorrow also distracted him. His mother's death in 1627 was a grievous blow. Physical weakness impeded even his scholarly pursuits. His poems entitled "Affliction" graphically describe this stage of his life, and he began to feel a profound sense of uselessness. For Herbert the spiritual life was never merely a personal, interior pursuit, but involved also service to others. It is that sense which lends particular poignancy to his life in the period 1625–1629. He certainly articulates that experience in his two poems entitled "Employment." The first of them concludes:

> I am no link of thy great chain,
> But all my companie is a weed.
> Lord place me in thy consort; give one strain
>   To my poore reed.

Nevertheless, in the midst of that difficult time he began to understand that if he were to be strong he must do His word, not read it only, that it was his own prideful insistence on his unworthiness that held him in thrall.

Two things then occurred that strengthened him in his commitment to follow the call wherever it might lead. He met, courted and, in 1629, married Jane Danvers, who proved to be a soul mate in his ministry, and a year later he received the cure of Bemerton St. Andrew and Fuggleston St. Peter. "Me thoughts I heard one calling, *Child!* / And I reply'd, *My Lord.*" He accepted the call and was ordained to the priesthood.

His poem "Aaron" which he places late in his manuscript describes well how he came to that moment:

> Holinesse on the head,
> Light and perfections on the breast,
> Harmonious bells below, raising the dead
> To leade them unto life and rest:
>   Thus are true Aarons drest.

Bemerton St. Andrew's near Salisbury where Herbert served (1630–1633).

Profanenesse in my head,
Defects and darknesse in my breast,
A noise of passions ringing me for dead
Unto a place where is no rest:
Poore priest thus am I drest.

Onely another head
I have, another heart and breast,
Another musick, making live not dead,
Without whom I could have no rest:
In him I am well drest.

Christ is my onely head,
My alone onely heart and breast,
My onely musick, striking me ev'n dead;
That to the old man I may rest,
And be in him new drest.

So holy in the head,
Perfect and light in my deare breast,
My doctrine tun'd by Christ, (who is not dead,
But lives in me while I do rest)
Come people; Aaron's drest.

Thus to Bemerton he went, not because he had overcome his own sense of unworthiness, but because he recognized in it the reply to the persistent call, to "subject mine to the will of Jesus my Master."

How sweetly doth *My Master* sound! *My Master!*
As Amber-greese leaves a rich sent
Unto the taster:
So do these words a sweet content,
An orientall fragrancie, *My Master!*
    —"The Odour.2 Cor.2.15"

2.

In contrast to Herbert's conflicted movement toward inevitable ordination, the calling of R. S. Thomas seems prosaic: there is no Thomas poem equivalent to Herbert's "The Collar." In his most distinctively autobiographical collection, *The Echoes Return Slow* (1988), a series of matching prose pieces and poems, he moved directly from a pairing about his years at University College, Bangor, to one on conducting the funeral of a child. Thomas did write often and eloquently of the tasks of ministry, specifically, of course, of ministry in small rural parishes. And, unlike Herbert, his ministry was a long one: forty-two years in five different rural parishes. Typical of the tone and perspective in his treatment of ministry is this pairing from *Echoes*...:

What had been blue shadows on a
longed-for horizon, traced on an inherited
background, were shown in time to contain
this valley, this village and a church built
with stones from the river, where the rectory
stood, plangent as a mahogany piano. The
stream was a bright tuning-fork in the
moonlight. The hay-fields ran with a dark
current. The young man was sent
unprepared to expose his ignorance of life in
a leafless pulpit.

I was vicar of large things
in a small parish. Small-minded
I will not say; there were depths
in some of them I shrank back
from, wells that the word 'God'
fell into and died away,
and for all I know is still
falling. Who goes for water
to such must prepare for a long
wait. Their eyes looked at me
and were the remains of flowers
on an old grave. I was there,
I felt, to blow on ashes
that were too long cold. Often,
when I thought they were about
to unbar to me, the draught
out of their empty places
came whistling, so that I wrapped
myself in the heavier clothing
of my calling, speaking of light and love
in the thickening shadows of their kitchens.

Thomas's poems about or references to the priesthood give a strong sense of the tasks to which he was called and of the strains of and obstacles to carrying out those tasks. If his words are sometimes sharp, he also showed a strong empathy for his parishioners and was clear about pastoral responsibilities. What we miss is Herbert's personal sense of Him who was doing the calling. We find no parallel to "Me thoughts I heard one calling, *Child!* / And I reply'd, *My Lord.*" We should note the tentativeness of "Me thoughts I heard," but even so that is more certainty on the subject than one will find in Thomas.

In *Laboratories of the Spirit* (1975), published three years before his retirement from the ministry, he included a poem "The Calling" which challenges any effort to understand his vocation:

And the word came — was it a god
spoke or a devil? — Go
to that lean parish; let them tread
on your dreams; and learn silence

is wisdom. Be alone with yourself
as they are alone in the cold room
of the wind. Listen to the earth
mumbling the monotonous song

of the soil: I am hungry, I
am hungry, in spite of the red dung
of this people. See them go
one by one through that dark door

with the crumpled ticket of your prayers
in their hands. Share their distraught
joy at the dropping of their inane
children. Test your belief

in spirit on their faces staring
at you, on beauty's surrender
to truth, on the soul's selling
of itself for a corner

by the body's fire. Learn the thinness
of the window that is
between you and life, and how
the mind cuts itself if it goes through.

A quality common to Thomas and Herbert is the provisional nature
of their poems. While the individual poems stand very well by themselves,
they gain in resonance when read against earlier and later poems. Like
"shards of brittle crazie glass" in a stained glass window (to borrow from
Herbert), the individual poems interact with one another to form greater
patterns. *The Temple* contains virtually all of Herbert's English poems.
Thus, the complementarity of his poems is easy enough to grasp. With
Thomas the reader can easily approach the individual collections, each
usually containing forty to sixty poems, assuming both an interactive and
an experimental quality. Indeed, the very name of the collection from
which "The Calling" comes underscores the tentative nature of each poem,
as do such collection titles as *Frequencies*, *Experimenting with an Amen*,
and *Ingrowing Thoughts*. But it is as true of the whole canon of his work
stretching over a half-century. The "echoes may return slow," but they
return and one's sense and appreciation of a single poem grows by listening for them.

Unlike Herbert, however, Thomas does not present us with a
finished product: a sequencing that itself describes the "many spiritual
conflicts between God and my soul." The major gathering of his work,
Collected Poems, 1945–1990, simply reproduces, with some exclusions, the
individual collections in chronological order. He omitted some poems

that he no longer found satisfactory and rearranged some of the ordering. (Thomas indicated that his son actually made the selections, though it is difficult to imagine the poet himself did not play some role.) Additionally, the volume does not have any selections from two collections, *Counterpoint* and *The Echoes Return Slow*—their suite-like character make such excerpting difficult—nor, of course, from collections published after 1990 except for one poem from *Mass for Hard Times* ("A Marriage" written in memory of his wife). As a whole, his work is larger, more protean and less systematic—though no less experiential. The experiences Thomas described were not only his own efforts to understand, to find meaning, to give meaning, but those of the people among whom he ministered. There is more here of the hardness of daily living, the sheer weight of the mundane, the narrowness of the human heart— and more too of the silence of God. That is hardly surprising since the silence of God, while Herbert too experienced it, was a dominant theme for Thomas.

But if God is silent, "Who put it into his head to be a candidate for Holy Orders?" Thomas addressed that question most directly in his autobiographical piece "Neb." In Welsh the title means literally "No One." Thomas originally wrote it in Welsh. A condensed version of it (omitting the segment in which Thomas dealt with the question of his calling) appeared in English in 1986 (*Contemporary Authors: Autobiographical Series* 4, 301–313) and was republished in William V. Davis, ed., *Miraculous Simplicity: Essays on R. S. Thomas* (1993). A translation of the full text was published in Jason Walford Davies, ed. and trans., *R. S. Thomas: Autobiographies* (1997).

> But who knows in what way a man's fate asserts itself? We are familiar with the story in the Bible about God calling Samuel, and consequently we perhaps think that we must hear God's voice calling fairly clearly, if we are supposed to do a particular thing. But on reflection, of course, it is obvious that choosing a vocation depends on many things [*Autobiographies*, p. 34].

The one of many things that appears most often in the remarks on the subject made by Thomas and others is the influence of his mother. Interestingly, in the introduction to his *A Choice of George Herbert's Verse*, Thomas quotes at length from Izaak Walton's description of the influence of Magdalen Herbert over her son. One senses that Thomas's own mother was less moved by piety than by a desire for respectability. In a 1995 interview Thomas remarked that his mother "obviously had these secret ambitions for me. I was at a malleable age in my teens and I didn't raise any resistance. God moves in mysterious ways." (Quoted in Justin Wintle, *Furious Interiors*, p.114. See also *Autobiographies*, pp. 34–35.)

The temptation is to regard his entry to the priesthood as almost incidental. The fact that he consciously chose to spend his entire career in the active ministry in small rural parishes and in that time published sixteen collections of poetry might make him appear as yet another example of the Anglican country clergyman settled into a comfortable cure, allowing him to pursue some scholarly or literary interest whether it be a treatise on butterflies or the writing of poetry. To yield to that temptation, however, fails to take seriously Thomas's own words in both prose and poetry. "God moves in mysterious ways": if he was not serious in saying that, then he was not serious about anything, and whatever one thinks about Thomas as poet or priest one cannot doubt his absorbing seriousness.

All the evidence is that he pursued his calling as priest (preacher, pastor, liturgist) with dedication and purpose. He did hold himself apart from the broader workings of the institutional church, largely avoiding clergy convocations and the like, yet within the parish he was diligent in his ministrations to the people. Conscious of the differences between the parishes he served, he tried to speak to the parishioners of each in ways that would connect with their experience. And in that work he was driven by the same urgency that informed so much of his poetry.

> After all, there is nothing more important than the relationship between man and God. Nor anything more difficult than establishing that relationship. Who is it that ever saw God? Who ever heard Him speak? We have to live virtually the whole of our lives in the presence of an invisible and mute God. But that was never a bar to anyone seeking to come into contact with Him. That is what prayer is ... [*Autobiographies*, p. 104].

Was he beloved by all his parishioners, remembered by them now as a saint who dwelt among them? Of course not: few clergy are. George Herbert apparently was remembered that way and probably deservedly so, but his parish ministry lasted only three years, not forty-two. Thomas calls his career in the parish ministry "insignificant," but it was too long and touched too many people to be that, and too many touched him. Again from *The Echoes Return Slow*:

The cure of souls! Congregations
tend to get older. There is no cure for old
age. And the old tend to be sick. When one
should be leading them on to peer into the
future, one is drawn back by them into the
past. The visitation of the sick! A ministry
more credible because more noticeable than
the cure of souls.

They keep me sober,
the old ladies
stiff in their beds,
mostly with pale eyes
wintering me.
Some are like blonde dolls
their joints twisted;
life in its brief play
was a bit rough
Some fumble
with thick tongues for words
and are deaf;
shouting their faint names
I listen;
they are far off,
the echoes return slow.

But without them,
without the subdued light
their smiles kindle,
I would have gone wild,
drinking earth's huge draughts
of joy and woe.

What matters, however, is not the effectiveness of his ministry, but
the importance of it in defining him. He accepted his ministry, not as a
convenience, but as the place he was supposed to be. In "Neb" he also
wrote: "Life is a pilgrimage, and if we do not succeed in coming a little
nearer to the truth, if we do not have a better comprehension of the nature
of God before reaching the end of the journey, why was it we started the
journey at all?" (p. 106). A priest finally is only a servant helping other pilgrims on the way.

The priest picks his way
Through the parish. Eyes watch him
From windows, from the farms;
Hearts wanting him to come near.
The flesh rejects him.

Women, pouring from the black kettle,
Stir up the whirling tea-grounds

Of their thoughts; offer him a dark
Filling in their smiling sandwich.

Priests have a long way to go.
The people wait for them to come
To them over the broken glass
Of their vows, making them pay
With their sweat's coinage for their correction.

He goes up a green lane
Through growing birches; lambs cushion
His vision. He comes slowly down
In the dark, feeling the cross warp
In his hands; hanging on it his thought's icicles.

'Crippled soul,' do you say? looking at him
From the mind's height; 'limping through life
On his prayers. There are other people
In the world, sitting at table
Contented, though the broken body
And the shed blood are not on the menu.'

'Let it be so,' I say. 'Amen and amen.'
                    —"The Priest," *Not That He Brought Flowers*

Not exactly the stuff of a seminary recruiting poster, yet it has the same
force as Herbert's concluding "And I reply'd, *My Lord*."

3.

Whatever else it is poetry is a craft, being a poet a work. Both George
Herbert and R. S. Thomas incarnate that idea.

Steeped in the classics, Herbert first demonstrated his command of
language through his public function as Orator of the University and his
poetry shows the same command — and sensitivity to sound and sense. As
poet he employed a variety of verse forms: there are 164 poems in *The
Temple*, each one different. Herbert was not simply being clever; rather he
used the range of his art to declare that all forms of poetry were servants
of the faith. Nor did he choose the forms serendipitously, but wedded them
to the sense of the poem. For example, "The Collar," which describes rebel-

liousness against the call of God, is free verse without rhymes and with seemingly erratic shifts of rhythm until the final four lines:

> But as I rav'd and grew more fierce and wilde
> > At every word,
> > Me thoughts I heard one calling, *Child!*
> > > And I reply'd, *My Lord.*

He further demonstrated his craftsmanship by the care he took in sequencing his poems. But, aside from this body of work, which remains a shining testament to his mind and heart and soul, we have little explicit evidence of what it meant to him to be a poet.

The closest he came to measured reflection on the matter was in the dedication which appeared in the manuscript and the subsequent printed versions, the first stanza of "The Church-porch" (the opening section of *The Temple*), references in particular poems (especially "Jordan (I)" and "The Forerunners") and his instructions to Nicholas Ferrar regarding the manuscript. The dedication reads:

> Lord, my first fruits present themselves to thee;
> > Yet not mine neither: for from thee they came,
> And must return. Accept of them and me,
> And make us strive, who shall sing best thy name.
> > Turn their eyes hither, who shall make a gain:
> > Theirs, who shall hurt themselves or me, refrain.

The premise that the fruits of his creativity were not merely of his own making, but came to him from God, is hardly surprising. Strikingly, he calls them his "first fruits," which suggests a particular valuing of them, and the fourth line underscores that valuation by both stressing the effort involved and defining as his purpose singing best the Lord's name. The final two lines lead naturally into the opening stanza of "The Church-porch":

> Thou, whose sweet youth and early hopes inhance
> > Thy rate and price, and mark thee for a treasure;
> Hearken unto a Verser, who may chance
> Ryme thee to good, and make a bait of pleasure.
> > A verse may find him, who a sermon flies,
> > And turn delight into a sacrifice.

To a degree the explanation of his purpose in the above-cited passages is formulaic, the affirmation of a common theme among seventeenth-century English religious poets. It was a necessary defense against the querulous question of certain Christians: why would a priest also be a poet? As Countryman argued, Herbert, with Donne and Vaughan, established the Anglican tradition of affinity between the two vocations.

Both "Jordan (I)" and "The Forerunners" speak more vigorously to that question. In the former he declares:

> Who sayes that fictions onely and false hair
> Become a verse? Is there in truth no beautie?
> Is all good structure in a winding stair?
> May no lines passe, except they do their dutie
>   Not to a true, but painted chair?
>
> Is it no verse, except enchanted groves
> And sudden arbours shadow course-spunne lines?
> Must purling streams refresh a lovers loves?
> Must all be vail'd, while he that reades, divines,
>   Catching the sense of two removes?
>
> Shepherds are honest people; let them sing:
> Riddle who list, for me, and pull for Prime:
> I envie no mans nightingale or spring;
> Nor let them punish me with losse of rime,
>   Who plainly say, *My God, My King.*

A variety of specific meanings here are possible. The title may suggest that as Jesus was baptized in the Jordan, so too poetry may be baptized and not left merely to the love poets. The second stanza may critique allegorical poetry, calling for simpler, clearer language. The final stanza may allude to the psalms, themselves great lyric poetry and, of course, Jesus's favored mode of prayer. But the general meaning is clear: poetry is an entirely appropriate mode of expression for matters spiritual — and a suitable work for a priest.

In "The Forerunners" Herbert considered his vocation as a poet in light of his increasing sense of mortality, wondering whether, as his body weakened, so would his ability to exercise his poetic gift. It was not a happy prospect to him, yet, even in the face of it, he professed "Thou art still my God" and affirmed what he had sought to do:

Farewell sweet phrases, lovely metaphors.
But will ye leave me thus? when ye before
Of stews and brothels onely knew the doores,
Then did I wash you with my tears, and more,
      Brought you to Church well drest and clad:
My God must have my best, ev'n all I had.

He had done, he would continue to do, the best that he could with his words. What mattered was not his own pleasure with them, but that he has dedicated them to God.

True beautie dwells on high: ours is a flame
      But borrow'd thence to light us thither.
Beautie and beauteous words should go together.

Thomas himself remarked of Herbert "There is too often the impression that the verse is being made subordinate to an idea, and not that the idea emerges naturally from the poetry" (*A Choice . . .*, p. 14). Yet Herbert's rhetorical control, the vitality of his language and images supplied by the variety of his interests—and one must say as well the freshness of his faith — raise the bulk of his efforts far beyond the merely didactic or pietistic.

Undeniably, Herbert saw all his work, and certainly a work so important to him that he characterized its results as his "first fruits," as serving God, for that was the calling behind all his roles. He was a poet as he was a priest because God called him to be so. That conviction informed his instructions to Ferrar: "If he can think it may turn to the advantage of any dejected poor soul, let it be made public: if not, let him burn it; for I and it are less than the least of God's mercies" (Walton, *Life*, p. 311). He has done his best with the gifts God gave him and if it is not enough, so be it. All that he has done is strive to serve God.

4.

We know substantially more about Thomas's understanding of what it means to be a poet and of the nature of poetry and the poetic craft, and we know it more explicitly, than we know Herbert's. Thomas dealt with those subjects in his autobiographical writings, in interviews and essays and addresses, in his introductions to selections of poems by Herbert, Edward Thomas, and Wordsworth, and in his poetry.

In "Neb" even before he posed the question "Who put it into his head to be a candidate for Holy Orders?" he asked "Was he preparing himself to be a poet? How can someone become a poet? From where did the desire to write verses come...?" (p. 32). The form of the questions is perhaps telling, yet he gave no real answer to them, merely reporting that he had written verses in college. And while he was curate at Chirk, he noted, "Under the influence of the beautiful and exciting country to the west he continued to write poetry..." (p. 44). In a lecture given at the University College at Swansea in 1963 Thomas observed:

> I suppose most men wish to tell others of their experiences. They gratify this wish mainly in talk, that endless noise which goes on in streets and buses and pubs. But some few have been born with the urge and the gift to write about their experiences in prose, fewer in poetry ["Words and the Poet," Sandra Anstey, ed., *R. S. Thomas. Selected Prose* (1995 edition), p. 65].

Becoming a poet thus appears as incidental, yet as inevitable, as becoming a priest. In Thomas's descriptions of being a poet, however, he made clear there was more to it than simply having the gift — just as there was more to being a priest. In the essay "The Making of a Poem" he declared:

> ... It is the actual *craft* of poetry which is important, and I think this must be said and adhered to.... If a poet realizes that it has been his privilege to have a certain gift in the manipulation of language (language being the supreme human manifestation), then he is obviously committed from the very beginning to a life-time of self discipline, struggle, disappointment, failure, with just possibly that odd success which is greater in his eyes than it probably is in the eyes of anybody else [*Selected Prose*, p. 86].

Being a poet is studying the works of other poets, observing the world around one, developing technique, struggling to balance sound and sense: "The people who are most likely to be inspired are the people who have had the most training and done the most work.... There is something deliberate about the poetic craft..." (p. 89).

> For the first twenty years you are still growing,
> Bodily that is; as a poet, of course,
> You are not born yet. It's the next ten
> You cut your teeth on to emerge smirking
> For your brash courtship of the muse.
> You will take seriously those first affairs
> With young poems, but no attachments

Formed then but come to shame you,
When love has changed to a grave service
Of a cold queen.
                    From forty on
You learn from the sharp cuts and jags
Of poems that have come to pieces
In your crude hands how to assemble
With more skill the arbitrary parts
Of ode or sonnet, while time fosters
A new impulse to conceal your wounds
From her and from a bold public,
Given to pry.
                    You are old now
As years reckon, but in that slower
World of the poet you are just coming
To sad manhood, knowing the smile
On her proud face is not for you.
                    —"To a Young Poet," *The Bread of Truth*

Being a poet is a gift, but not necessarily a blessing, for it is a gift that requires long and diligent labor if one is to fulfill the obligation that the gift entails. "Words," one of the final poems in *No Truce with the Furies* (1995), begins "Accuse me of sincerity / I deny complicity / art is my necessity." God works in mysterious ways.

5.

While Herbert may have felt compelled to justify why he would address religious questions in poetry, Thomas more often had to confront the question why would a poet address religious questions. In our day, the term "religious poetry" has a dismissive quality to it akin, in the minds of some, to saying "He writes limericks." Following Thomas's death in September, 2000, many of the obituaries characterized him as a "poet of rural Wales" or a "Welsh nationalist," thus not only ignoring the breadth of his work, but also its fundamentally religious quality as if it were an embarrassment that he pursued so relentlessly questions of God and faith. Such an attitude, however, says more about the paucity of the modern imagination than it does about either poetry or religion.

To reiterate Williams's comment in *The English Poetic Mind*, "Religious poetry is poetry, not religion. But good poetry does something more than allude to its subject; it is related to it, and it relates us to it" (p. 3).

Søren Kierkegaard (in whose works Thomas read widely and deeply) wrote: "For life is like a poet, and on that account is different from the observer who always seeks to bring things to a conclusion. The poet pulls us into the very complex center of life" (*Purity of Heart*, p. 101). For both Herbert and Thomas that center was the relationship between man and God. One may argue against that conviction, but one cannot deny its creative force.

Thomas in his introduction to *The Penguin Book of Religious Verse* (1963) asked:

> What is the common ground between religion and poetry? Is there such? Do definitions help? If I say that religion is the total response of the whole person to reality, but poetry the response of a certain kind of person, I appear to be doing so at the expense of poetry. Perhaps Coleridge can help us here. The nearest we approach to God, he appears to say, is as creative beings. The poet by echoing the primary imagination, recreates.
>
> Through his work he forces those who read him to do the same, thus bringing them nearer the primary imagination themselves, and so, in a way, nearer to the actual being of God as displayed in action…. Now the power of the imagination is a unifying power, hence the force of metaphor; and the poet is the supreme manipulator of metaphor. This would dispose of him as a minor craftsman among many. The world needs the unifying power of the imagination. The two things which give it best are poetry and religion … [pp. 8–9].

Poetry concerns itself with the concrete and particular, not to simplify, but to elucidate. Given the limitations of human understanding, the imperfections of language itself, poetry enables us to think about, speak about, grapple with "The complex center of life." For Herbert it was the natural and obvious way to record "the many spiritual conflicts which passed betwixt God and my soul." As James Boyd White observed, "The central drama of Herbert's verse lies in its ways of imagining God, and the speaker and the relation between them…." ("*This Book of Starres.*", p. 194). In the introduction to his selection of Herbert poems, Thomas was more specific: "Yeats said that out of his quarrel with others a man makes rhetoric, but out of his quarrel with himself poetry. Herbert surely had no quarrel with others. What he had was an argument, not with others, nor with himself primarily, but with God, and God always won" (p. 12). Above all else the argument was about his calling. Both poetry and priesthood are vocations of the word. By being a poet Herbert was able to describe the argument.

Which is not to say there is no tension between the two vocations. In one of the prose/poem pairings in *Echoes …*, Thomas wrote:

Salving his conscience in the face of
the Gospel's commandment to judge not
with the necessity for the writer of poetry to
be his own critic. The creative mind judges,
weighs and selects, as well as discarding, in
the act of composing. Yet honesty is
without mercy, punishing the practitioner
along with the patient.

What I ask of humans
is more than human
so without idolatry
I can follow. While he,

who is called God, now
scorches with sparks of
blood, now glaciates me
in the draught out of his tomb.

Later he noted, "He defended himself with the fact that Jesus was a poet."

Thomas finally saw poetry as the best literary form "to express or convey religious truth.... Religion has to do first of all with vision, revelation, and these are best told in poetry" ("A Frame for Poetry," *Selected Prose*, p. 69). In saying this, Thomas spoke not only within the Anglican tradition, but also within the deep stream of the Welsh bardic tradition in which the tasks of the poet and of the priest seem closely allied. In his study of that tradition, A. M. Allchin has observed, "We could say as truly that man is called to be a priest and a poet, one who under God and with God is called to be a creator" (*Praise Above All. Discovering the Welsh Tradition*, Cardiff, 1991, p. 7). Allchin subsequently commented that much of his argument "could be read as providing a background to his [Thomas's] work" (p. 159).

In a television interview Thomas remarked "Primarily I'm trying to find out what it means to use the word 'God' in the late twentieth century with all the discoveries and changes which have come about in the human intellect." That observation sums up not only the central preoccupation of Thomas as poet, but also the difference between Thomas and Herbert, a difference primarily of time and opportunity. We live within our experience that both enables us and limits us. Of Herbert, Thomas stated: "[He] demonstrates ... both the possibility and the desirability of a friendship with God. Friendship is no longer the right way to describe it. The word now is dialogue, encounter, confrontation; but the realities engaged have not altered all that much" (*A Choice ...*, p. 16). If anything Thomas grew more uncomfortable over the years with the idea of a "friendship with God." How can one establish a friendship or even a dialogue with one of whom your primary experience is silence?

In a late poem, "Resurrections" (*No Truce ...*), Thomas spoke directly of those poets with whom he has been most often identified and in so doing gives weight to that question:

Easier for them, God
only at the beginning
of his recession. Blandish him,
said the times and they did so,
Herbert, Traherne, walking
in a garden not yet
polluted. Music in Donne's
mind was still polyphonic.

The corners of the spirit waiting
to be developed, Hopkins
renewed the endearments
taming the lion-like presence
lying against
him. What
happened? Suddenly he was
gone, leaving love guttering
in his withdrawal. And scenting
disaster, as flies are attracted
to a carcase, far down
in the subconscious the ghouls
and the demons we thought
we had buried for ever resurrected.

Yet Thomas also remarked of Herbert: "He commends a way of life for the individual that is still viable. It is reason, not so much tinged with, as warmed by emotion, and solidly based on order and discipline, the soul's good form" (p. 17). Being a Christian is like being a poet: committed "to a life-time of self discipline, struggle, disappointment, failure, with just possibly that odd success which is greater in his eyes than it probably is in the eyes of anybody else." And being a poet is like being a Christian.

In an essay written shortly after Thomas's death, John Pikoulis observed that rather than speaking of him as "poet and priest" a more accurate term would be "poet but priest" in recognition of the fact that they "pulled apart in him as often as they pulled together" ("Remembering R. S. Thomas," *New Welsh Review*, Winter 2000–2001, p. 5). In a television interview with Jon Ormond in 1972, however, Thomas had emphatically connected his vocations, declaring "poetry is religion, religion is poetry" (for a transcript of the interview see *Poetry Wales*, Spring, 1972, pp. 47–57). Even so, Thomas clearly had more doubts about his priestly vocation than his poetic one, but those very doubts fed and enriched his poetry — just as doubts fed and enriched Herbert's art. Finally, however, for both being a poet was an extension of his calling. Certainly Thomas argued with others and persistently with himself, but time and again he returned to the argument with God which gave all else force.

> Why, then, of all possible
> turnings do we take
> this one rather than that,
> when the only signs discernible
> are what no one has erected?
> Is it because, at the road's
> ending, the one who is as a power
> in hiding is waiting to be christened?
> —"The Waiting," *No Truce with the Furies*, p. 64

II

"A Little Aside from the Main Road": Country Parsons

In commenting on Herbert's and Thomas's sense of calling to the priesthood, I have made it clear that both followed that calling with high seriousness. And, in their poetry, they gave us some sense of the challenging dailiness of serving rural parishes. In that regard Thomas provided a more graphic picture both because his experience was far longer and because, while Herbert focused on the waywardness of the Christian pilgrimage, Thomas was rather an observer seeking to make sense of the world around him ("I am eyes / Merely ...," *H'm*, 1972, p. 2).

Herbert described parish ministry more in terms of what it ought to be as he confronted human weaknesses and shortcomings; Thomas described it as it was in its daily tasks. As if to underscore that distinction, Herbert left behind him, in addition to the manuscript of his poems, a prose work (*The Country Parson. His Character and Rule of Holy Life*) which set forth the "Form and Character of a true Pastour." Not surprisingly, we have no such document from Thomas: the seventeenth century was a time far more conducive to and productive of such manuals. What we have is an early, extended poem, *The Minister*, that in a *via negativa* illustrates the ideals Herbert elaborates. To compare the two works may well be the proverbial comparison of apples and oranges, yet it is, I think, instructive.

1.

Like his poetry, *The Country Parson* was not published until after Herbert's death. While the poems were published in at least fifteen editions between 1633 and 1709, *The Country Parson* appeared in only four editions between 1652 and 1701. Although it has some appeal in itself, its primary interest was and is as a work by the poet of *The Temple*. As my own references suggest, it is certainly a helpful document in illustrating Herbert's character and beliefs. In his preface to the work, Herbert wrote:

> Being desirous (thorow the Mercy of God) to please Him, for whom I am, and live, and who giveth me my Desires and Performances; and considering with my self, That the way to please him, is to feed my Flocke diligently and faithfully, since our Saviour hath made that the argument of a Pastour's love, I have resolved to set down the Form and Character of a true Pastour, that I may have a Mark to aim at: which also I will set as high as I can, since he shoots higher that threatens the Moon, then hee that aims at a Tree. Not that I think, if a man do not all that is here expressed, hee presently sinns, and displeases God, but that it is a good strife to go as farre as wee can in pleasing of him, who hath done so much for us.

Herbert would never have claimed for himself that he "hit the mark." Indeed, as we have seen in discussing his sense of calling, he long struggled with a conviction of his own unworthiness. Even after going to Bemerton and being ordained to the priesthood, he would have said of himself, not that he was worthy, but that he had aligned his will with God's and would serve as He desired. What we know of him from others, however, suggests, as Nicholas Ferrar wrote in his preface to *The Temple*, that he was "justly a companion to the primitive Saints, and a pattern or more for the age he lived in"—and later ones as well.

Thomas originally wrote *The Minister* for broadcast as part of a series of "Radio Odes" over the Welsh Home Service. It was aired on September 18, 1952, and published in 1953. It is a mini verse drama with four voices: a narrator, the minister (the Reverend Elias Morgan), the head of the chapel vestry (Job Davies), and a young woman (Buddug). Thomas was not describing any of the Church in Wales parishes he served, but rather a small rural, nonconformist chapel, probably in the hills above Manafon. Thus while some of its qualities are merely rural, some are rooted in the particular ethos of Welsh Calvinism or Calvinistic Methodism.

In that regard one of the important differences is the way in which a minister is called to a church. Herbert received the living of Bemerton St. Andrew's and Fulston St. Peter by royal appointment and the concurrence of the Earl of Pembroke. This gave him an independence which allowed him easily to say of the parson's relation to the parish wardens, "The Country Parson doth often, both publicly, and privately instruct his Church-Wardens what a great Charge lies upon them, and that indeed the whole order and discipline of the Parish is put into their hands" (p. 269). Herbert emphasized the responsibility of the parson in inviting and attracting good men to this office.

In contrast, the chapel vestry in *The Minister* has the power of appointment and

> They chose their pastors as they chose their horses
> For hard work. But the last one died
> Sooner than they expected; nothing sinister,
> You understand, but just the natural
> Breaking of the heart beneath a load
> Unfit for horses. 'Ay, he's a good 'un,'
> Job Davies had said; and Job was a master
> Hand at choosing a nag or a pastor.

And Job has a clear prescription for the new minister:

> A young 'un we want, someone young
> Without a wife. Let him learn
> His calling first, and choose after
> Among our girls, if he must marry.

Job underscores his argument by pointing out the problems another one of the chapel deacons had when he bought a mare that was too old, spoiled by the "taste of the valleys" and unable to adjust to the rough hill grass and to the work.

> Lucky you sold her. But you can't sell
> Ministers, so we must have a care
> In choosing. Take my advice,
> Pick someone young, and I'll soon show him
> How things is managed in the hills here.

Between the two processes for appointment — selection by a patron, whether ecclesiastical or secular, and selection by a congregational vestry — neither can be said to be superior except in terms of convictions about church polity or social order. Herbert himself clearly accepted the social assumptions of his day: in his instruction about selecting Church wardens he declared, "The Parson suffers not the place to be vilified or debased, by being cast on the lower rank of people." One hardly need say that the assumption that the social elite better serve the interests of God and church is flawed, but, of course, Herbert operated within the social structure and assumptions of his time. In any case, he was not arguing about church polity; rather he was "setting a high mark" to define his own responsibilities within the parish. Nor was Thomas making an argument about church polity. Instead, he was describing the rough realities of a rural congregation that set the conditions for the story of the Reverend Elias Morgan.

2.

Young and unmarried, as Job Davies desired, the Reverend Elias Morgan, B. A., came to the hill country bright-eyed and eager. In a deft portrait spoken by Morgan himself, Thomas limned the qualities that would bring him to grief:

> My cheeks were pale and my shoulders bowed
> With years of study, but my eyes glowed
> With a deep, inner phthisic zeal,
> For I was the lamp which the elders chose
> To thaw the darkness that had congealed
> About the hearts of the hill folk.
> I wore a black coat, being fresh from college,
> With striped trousers, and, indeed, my knowledge
> Would have been complete, had it included
> The bare moor, where nature brooded
> Over her old, inscrutable secret.
> But I didn't even know the names
> Of the birds and the flowers by which one gets
> A little closer to nature's heart.

The term "phthisic zeal" is telling. It announces the latent consumption that afflicts and finally will kill him and defines his frailty amidst this rugged land and people. But the choice of words also manifests his separation, his isolation from the hill folk. He hardly talks their language, nor does he really see their world, nor recognize what he must learn. The sound of the thrush troubles him; he sees the evening sunlight as a temptation. His self-appointed mentor could be of no help, for Job Davies sees his task as showing him "how things is managed in the hills here." However, that is not a commitment to rouse the young minister to an appreciation of the natural world, but to bind him to the narrow ways of men. The term suggests as well the tenuous nature of Morgan's zeal: it is all inner, rooted in book learning and a faith driven by a preoccupation with a judgmental God, a consumptive fire that will exhaust itself.

Herbert's prescription for what a country parson should know makes clear Morgan's deficiencies:

> The Country Parson is full of all knowledge. They say, it is an ill Mason that refuseth any stone: and there is no knowledge, but, in a skilful hand, serves either positively as it is, or else to illustrate some other knowledge. He condescends even to the knowledge of tillage, and pastorage, and makes great use of them in teaching, because people by what they understand, are best led to what they understand not [p. 228].

He added that the parson should study those human activities which "are most incident to his parish." He also advised him to use his weekday afternoons to visit around the parish so that he might see his parishioners in the midst of their daily lives, so better to understand them and how to approach them.

The argument is a pragmatic one, but it is also rooted in Herbert's appreciation for the natural world. Nature is worth attending to, not simply as a strategy for ministry, but as an avowal of God as the Creator of all things. In contrast, Morgan, seeing the few flowers blooming beneath his window, thinks them untidy and pulled them up: "He sprinkled cinders there instead."

Morgan never understands nature as a part of God' intention; it is always something other, alien, not friendly. He preaches not the God of Creation, but the God of Judgment and this act of pulling up the flowers and sprinkling cinders becomes a metaphor of his ministry. Through the narrator's voice, Thomas followed the description of that action with a description of Morgan preaching.

> Who is this opening and closing the Book
> With a bang, and pointing a finger
> Before him in accusation?
> Who is this leaning from the wide pulpit
> In judgment, and filling the chapel
> With sound as God fills the sky?

He excites the people with the passion of his delivery, "Except for the elders, and even they were moved / By the holy tumult, but not extremely. / They knew better than that." But the results are the opposite of what he intended.

It was sex, sex, sex and money, money,
God's mistake and the devil's creation,
That took the mind of the congregation
On long journeys into the hills
Of a strange land, where sin was the honey
Bright as sunlight in death's hive.
They lost the parable and found the story,
And their glands told them they were still alive.
Job looked at Buddug, and she at him
Over the pews, and they knew they'd risk it
Some evening when the moon was low.

Disconnected from the land and the people, Morgan's flame is fed entirely by his abstract learning rather than experience. He speaks of expounding the Word, which gives a different sense than Herbert's advice to the parson to select texts of devotion.

In his chapter "The Parson preaching," Herbert reiterated that the parson must be sensitive to his congregation, know to whom he speaks, and in fact vary his manner and delivery so he, in effect, talks in turn to the individuals. "This is for you, and This for you; for particulars ever touch, and awake more than generalls." Above all, he emphasized that "The character of his Sermon is Holiness; he is not learned, or witty, or eloquent, but Holy."

Morgan goes away from the service happy with himself, with his eloquence and delivery:

I was good that night, I had the *hwyl.*
We sang the verses of the last hymn
Twice. We might have had a revival
If only the organ had kept in time.
But that was the organist's fault.
I went to my house with the light heart
Of one who had made a neat job
Of pruning the branches on the tree
Of good and evil.

He holds a fellowship meeting, but no one comes. They tell him that it is lambing time or haying time or time to gather peat. These are excuses— and also evidence of his isolation from, lack of understanding of, the patterns of their lives. Winter is the time for such meetings, they tell him. He holds a Bible study, but only a girl "not right in the head" comes. Of a summer evening he thinks of visiting, but "it more often seems / That bed is the shorter path to the friendlier morrow." The ephemeral effect of his preaching is all too evident.

He leaves on holiday and returns refreshed. However, the mood hardly survives a few months. The old pallor comes back to his cheeks: "In his long fight / with the bare moor it was the moor that was winning." The Sunday school children play tricks on him. He retreats to the pulpit, "a kind of block house / From which to fire the random shot / Of innuendo," a spirit the very antithesis of Herbert's ideal. Yet something like courage, which is also foolishness, leads Morgan to speak to Job Davies about his relationship with Buddug. Davies, one can imagine with narrowed eyes and steely gaze, responds:

> Adultery's a big word, Morgan: where's your proof?
> You who never venture from under your roof
> Once the night's come; the blinds all down
> For fear of the moon's bum rubbing the window.
> Take a word from me and keep your nose
> In the black Book, so it won't be tempted
> To go sniffing where it's not wanted.
> And leave us farmers to look to our own
> Business, in case the milk goes sour
> From your sharp talk before it's churned
> To good butter, if you see what I mean.

The rebuttal is arrogant and threatening: part of Morgan's living depends on gifts-in-kind from Davies. It also reflects Job's sly intelligence, for he attacks where Morgan is most vulnerable, his failures to learn the parish and to connect with nature.

Herbert spoke strongly of the Parson's responsibility to correct those who go astray, but of course the legal authority of a parson in a seventeenth-century Anglican parish was very different from that of a twentieth-century free church minister. Again, however, Herbert insisted that the effectiveness of the parson in correcting his people depends on understanding the realities of the life that they lead. In a chapter entitled "The Parson's eye," he described the need to observe, but he also showed a profounder understanding of sin than Morgan does. Parsons, he observed, should have "exactly sifted the definitions of all vertues, and vices" and have connected rules of conduct "to the smallest actions of Life; which while they dwell in their bookes, they will never finde." Herbert was sensitive to the sins of human beings; Morgan does battle with Sin. Thus when he ventures to speak with Davies he fails.

Davies has completed his task; he has made Morgan understand "how things is managed in the hills here." Morgan is tamed to the plough.

> I was the chapel pastor, the abrupt shadow
> Staining the neutral fields, troubling the men
> Who grew there with my glib, dutiful praise
> Of a fool's world; a man ordained for ever
> To pick his way along the grass-strewn wall
> Dividing tact from truth.
>   I knew it all,
> Although I never pried, I knew it all.
> I knew why Buddug was away from chapel.
> I knew that Pritchard, the *Fron*, watered his milk.
> I knew who put the ferret with the fowls
> In Pugh's hen-house. I knew and pretended I didn't.
> And they knew that I knew and pretended I didn't.
> They listened to me preaching the unique gospel
> Of love; but our eyes never met. And outside
> The blood of God darkened the evening sky.

This corruption of soul mingles with the corruption lurking in his lungs. He sickens and dies. The chapel vestry, no doubt, will go looking for another young one.

3.

The story of Elias Morgan is a bleak one, but Thomas, who understood well the challenges of ministry in rural Wales, also knew that there were good men laboring in those vineyards, that there are small victories of faith and moments of epiphany in the hills and valleys. In contrast to the description of Morgan preaching quoted above, we have "The Chapel":

> A little aside from the main road,
> becalmed in a last-century greyness,
> there is the chapel, ugly, without the appeal
> to the tourist to stop his car
> and visit it. The traffic goes by,
> and the river goes by, and quick shadows
> of clouds, too, and the chapel settles
> a little deeper into the grass.

But here once on an evening like this,
in the darkness that was about
his hearers, a preacher caught fire
and burned steadily before them
with a strange light, so that they saw
the splendour of the barren mountains
about them and sang their amens
fiercely, narrow but saved
in a way that men are not now.
                              —*Laboratories of the Spirit*

Morgan's zeal rouses the minds of his listeners "to long journeys into the hills / of a strange land." This anonymous preacher brings his parishioners to see more vividly the world around them. C. S. Lewis, in delineating what he meant by true joy, emphasized its power to light up "the splendour of the barren mountains," that is the things we see daily. "Up till now," he wrote, "each visitation of Joy had left the common world momentarily a desert.... But now I saw the bright shadow coming ... into the real world and resting there, transforming all common things..." (*Surprised by Joy*, p. 181). Lewis's observation catches something of the quality which this preacher imparts. Herbert insisted that what should characterize a parson's sermons above all is holiness. It is the fire of holiness that casts the "bright shadow" that makes all things new, that is the "strange light" enabling us to see "the splendour of the mountains." All poor Morgan has is his "phthisic zeal"—which he mistook for something more.

In "The Country Clergy" (*Poetry for Supper*) Thomas wrote:

I see them working in old rectories
By the sun's light, by candlelight,
Venerable men, their black cloth
A little dusty, a little green
With holy mildew. And yet their skulls,
Ripening over so many prayers,
Toppled into the same grave
With oafs and yokels. They left no books,
Memorial to their lonely thought
In grey parishes; rather they wrote
On men's hearts and in the minds
Of young children sublime words
Too soon forgotten. God in his time
Or out of time will correct this.

In this poem and the later "Country Cures" (*The Bread of Truth*) and "The Priest" (*Not That He Brought Flowers*), Thomas delineated lives of tedious devotion and service. They seem to differ from Morgan's only in the way the preacher in "The Chapel" differs from him: they know the world in which they dwell. And that is enough: Thomas wrote of such clergy without making them more than they were, but also without demeaning them.

And why should he: he was one of them. Throughout *The Echoes Return Slow* Thomas writes candidly of the tensions involved in the life of a parish priest who must study and pray and minister to men and women whose daily existence is worlds away from "the study, that puzzle to the farm mind." Herbert understood those tensions as well, but in his poems he does not speak specifically of them, only of his difficulties in bearing the burdens of priesthood. But he persevered, as did Thomas.

It was at St. Michael and All Angels, Manafon, that Thomas began seriously to engage those tensions and in the process to recognize the sturdy and durable virtues of God's people. He not only ministered to them, but they to him. The result was the poetic that emerged in his early collections. In 1960, W. Moelwyn Merchant observed, "His priest's vocation is never obtruded in the verse, ... but I doubt if the verse would exist at all — it would certainly not have this ascetic spareness— but for his cure of souls" (*Critical Quarterly*, II.4, Winter 1960, pp. 345–346).

In an uncollected poem that appeared in *Poetry Wales* (VI.1, Summer 1970), Thomas writes:

> Mine is the good cause
> If lost. I revolve still
> Among persons, give them names,
> Join, bury them.
>
> One comes into the world
> Like a violet, so soft
> The unseeing eyes. I brush
> With water, the Church's
> Sublime dew. He grows tall,
> Absent; but will return
> Soon with his bride, asking
> The favour of the candles
> And music.
>
> Always
> They go, and always

The hole in the ground waits.
The stone pages go on
With their story. God, I
tell them, will read this. Together
We mend the edges of
Our amens. The planes roar
in the sky. Science repeats
Its promises. Against times
That infect I offer my
priceless inoculation.
                    —"Vocation"

Perhaps, in the twentieth and now the twenty-first centuries, such lives, such vocations as these, seem peripheral, insignificant, when viewed from "the mind's height," but Thomas closes "The Priest" with the benediction, "'Let it be so,' I say. 'Amen and amen.'"

   In *The Country Parson* Herbert set a high standard, yet he made clear it was a mark to shoot for, not one easily (or perhaps ever) attained. Conscious of his own frailties, he certainly never claimed to have reached it, though, again, others might claim it for him. But he also believed that "God doth often vessels make / Of lowly matter for high uses meet ..." ("The Priesthood"). It was the striving that mattered: "Not that I think, if a man do not all that is here expressed, hee presently sinns, and displeases God, but that it is a good strife to go as farre as wee can in pleasing of him, who hath done so much for us." Knowing that, he, too, could say for himself and for other servants of the servants of God, "'Let it be so,' I say. 'Amen and amen.'"

III

The Word and the Poets: The Bible

As poets George Herbert and R. S. Thomas were men of words; as priests they were preachers of the Word. Again, religious poetry is poetry, not religion, but necessarily the words they used, the images they invoked, including words and images drawn directly from or alluding to the Bible, come laden with meanings and implications inherent in the religious tradition they shared. To be sure, they were separated by more than three centuries and by changes that in some cases have complicated, and in others attenuated those meanings and implications. Certainly, the post-Enlightenment tradition of biblical criticism made it difficult for Thomas to view the Bible in the same way as Herbert. Thomas was necessarily more allusive, suggestive, in his treatment. However, that quality came not, or not merely, from a different attitude towards the Bible. It came also from the fact that Herbert's central poetic work, *The Temple*, is a finished depiction of the Christian's spiritual journey, while the larger, more discursive, body of Thomas's poetry is a series of impressionistic images of a pilgrim in a strange land, a land where the sense of God's absence, of man's loneliness, of the necessity of waiting, is pervasive.

1.

For Herbert, the scriptures were a living, vibrant document. He lived in the glow of the appearance of the new translation of the Bible, the King James Version, which has had powerful religious and literary effects on English cultural history. Yet, he lived as well in a time when controversy and violence over words and phrases in the scriptures was commonplace. Steeped in classical learning, adept in both Latin and Greek, and experienced in the art of translating both ancient and modern texts, he was well equipped both to appreciate the achievements of the men who prepared the authorized version and to understand the complexities and challenges of translating the Scriptures into contemporary language. However divinely guided, the translation, as Herbert well knew, was the product of a distinctly human intellectual (and political) process.

Except for this special sensitivity to language, Herbert's view of the Bible was hardly unusual for his time. As a priest of the established church, he accepted Article VI of the Articles of Religion: "Holy Scripture containeth all things necessary to salvation: so that whatsoever is not read therein, nor may be proved thereby, is not to be required of any man, that it should be believed as an article of the Faith, or be thought requisite or necessary to salvation." This is not a statement asserting biblical literalism. Rather it affirms that the Bible is the core document from which Christians learn the Faith.

But if his view of the scriptures was commonplace, his affirmation of that view has his typical eloquence. In chapter four of *The Country Parson*, speaking of a priest's requisite learning, he affirmed, "... The chief and top of his knowledge consists in the book of books, the storehouse and magazene of life and comfort, the holy Scriptures. There he sucks, and lives. In the Scriptures hee findes four things; Precepts for life, Doctrines for knowledge, Examples for illustration, and Promises for comfort." He was not merely stating efficacious theory, but was describing his own daily experience with the Bible. In chapter seven, delineating the responsibilities of the parson as preacher, he emphasized the need to select "texts of Devotion, not Controversie, moving and ravishing texts, whereof the Scriptures are full." The pulpit, then, is not a platform for theological debate or doctrinal fulminations or "crumbling a text into small parts," but for drawing people closer to the life God would have them lead.

The first of his two poems on the Bible seems a rendering in poetic language of the thoughts expressed in *The Country Parson*:

> Oh Book! Infinite sweetnesse! Let my heart
>   Suck ev'ry letter, and a hony gain,
>   Precious for any grief in any part;
> To cleare the breast, to mollifie all pain.
> Thou art all health, health thriving till it make
>   A full eternitie: thou art a masse
>   Of strange delights, where we may wish & take.
> Ladies, look here; this is the thankfull glasse,
> That mends the lookers eyes: this is the well
>   That washes what it shows. Who can indeare

> Thy praise too much? Thou art heav'ns Lidger here,
> Working against the states of death and hell.
> Thou art joyes handsell: heav'n lies flat in thee,
> Subject to ev'ry mounters bended knee.
> —"The H. Scriptures I"

Here we have "four things; Precepts for life, Doctrines for knowledge, Examples for illustration, and Promises for comfort." The form is declamatory, directed to the source of these benefits, though with the distinctive shift in address in lines eight to ten from the scriptures themselves to "Ladies." That shift, however, only serves to emphasize the essential thrust of the poem as a song of praise.

Though the closest he came to identifying the Bible as the Word of God is the phrase "heav'ns Lidger," he addressed the Bible almost as a person — in much the same voice as so many of his poems address God. Additionally, instead of describing the Bible by its contents, he did so with a series of terms and phrases that emphasize its effect: "a masse of strange delights," "the thankfull glass," "the well that washes," "heav'ns Lidger," "joyes handsell."

All these highlight the conviction that the Bible is "the storehouse and magazene of life and comfort," and that the reading of the Bible should be part of one's daily devotion — as it was of Herbert's. The reading itself cannot be a casual endeavor, but is a spiritual exercise, for the Scriptures can only be understood "with the same Spirit that writ them."

The second poem, yoked with the first as if it were merely the second stanza of a single poem, assumes the first, yet by itself has a distinctiveness and personal quality that transcends it. To be sure, it too contains an element of praise, including the phrase "This book of starres," which is even more elegant and eloquent than any of the descriptive terms he employed in the first poem. Herbert also said something of the effects of the Scriptures, though more specifically on himself. But the central theme of the poem is the nature of the Bible.

> Oh that I knew how all thy lights combine,
>   And the configurations of their glorie!
>   Seeing not onely how each verse doth shine,
> But all the constellations of the storie.
> This verse marks that, and both do make a motion
>   Unto a third, that ten leaves off doth lie:
>   Then as dispersed herbs do watch a potion,
> These three make up some Christian destinie:

Such are thy secrets, which my life makes good,
        And comments on thee: for in ev'ry thing
        Thy words do finde me out, & parallels bring,
And in another make me understood.
        Starres are poor books, & oftentimes do misse:
        This book of starres lights to eternall blisse.
                                    —"The H. Scriptures II"

In his introduction to *The Penguin Book of Religious Verse*, R. S. Thomas observed, "The nearest we approach to God, ... [Coleridge says], is as creative beings. The poet, by echoing the primary imagination, recreates. Through his work he forces those who read him to do the same, thus bringing them nearer the primary imagination themselves, and so, in a way, nearer to the actual being of God as displayed in action" (Thomas, *Selected Prose*, p. 64). In another essay, "A Frame for Poetry," Thomas emphasized the essentially poetic nature of the Bible (p. 90). As a poet Herbert knew the power of words; he also knew their limitations. He understood then the necessity of metaphor and allusion in order to make meanings either more precise or more expansive. One must also note that Herbert consistently used puns, that is, intentionally evoked double meanings.

In this second poem, he began with the awed wish that he knew how the Scriptures worked, in effect, poetically. Implicit is the assumption that one cannot apprehend biblical truth simply by defining words, one of the ways we have of "crumbling a text into small parts." What matters are not individual points of light, "but all the constellations of the storie." Explicit is the conviction that biblical truth reveals itself, not through the dissection of phrases on a page, but through the lives of people of the Word. Again, as he declared in *The Country Parson*: "The character of his Sermon is Holiness: he is not witty, or learned, or eloquent, but Holy" (p. 233). And the holiness of the preacher is inseparable from his life. "Such are thy secrets, which my life makes good, / And comments on thee." As noted before Herbert addressed the Bible as if it were a person and in effect it is, the Living Word in which we too must live and move and have our being.

Taken together the two poems manifest the characteristic movement of Herbert's poesy: praise of God and His gifts to us, proclamation that those gifts must show forth in our lives, confession of his inadequacy, and finally wondering recognition that, even so, the constellation of God's grace shone on him.

A discussion of these poems hardly exhausts Herbert's references to and uses of Scripture for they suffuse the whole body of his work. Clearly one of the ways in which *The Temple* coheres is through the recurrence and resonance of biblical language and imagery, which, in a sense, provide the mortar for the blocks of the poems themselves. In her *Spelling the Word: George Herbert and the Bible* (Berkeley, 1985), Chana Bloch argued that "if we take as our guide the Bible, we can come closest to the very center of *The Temple*." Her point is well taken though Herbert is not unique among the religious poets of the seventeenth century in this regard. The Bible was the central source of the shared cultural experience of both the poets and their readers. Thus biblical language and imagery pervaded the writing of Herbert, Vaughan, Traherne, and others. As Countryman observed, "It becomes a language for conversation with God" (*The Poetic Imagination*, p. 38). Bloch's title is drawn from a line in Herbert's "The Flower": "Thy word is all, if we could spell." As she points out, "spell" means "learning to understand and do." Herbert's poems manifest his own learning to spell God's word and offer a guide to others in that task.

2.

As noted, among the things separating Thomas from Herbert was the chasm of modern biblical criticism. Which is not to say that Thomas necessarily accepted or incorporated the results of that scholarship into his poetry, but he knew it was there: it is part of the atmosphere of our times. Yet he asserted even more directly than Herbert that one cannot grasp the nettle of biblical truth by reductive analysis. Only the poetic imagination offers the means of approaching it, though never fully, never finally, for metaphor remains approximate and the human mind is imperfect.

Though he spent his entire active ministry in rural Wales, Thomas did not write a version of *The Country Parson*. Still, Thomas's autobiographical writings and his poems about or referring to the priesthood provide a strong sense of the tasks to which he was called and of the strains of and obstacles to carrying out those tasks. If his words were sometimes sharp, he also showed a genuine empathy for his parishioners. And, like Herbert, his own life and ministry affirmed the necessity of a daily discipline that included prayer and the reading of Scripture.

That necessity informed his lack of enthusiasm for the idea that we must continually update the liturgy and prepare new translations of the Bible. His reasoning was both practical and poetic. In practical terms he argued that, whatever might be gained intellectually from the contemporary language, we lose in our devotional lives because the words are no longer common and customary, no longer instinctive to us. In poetic terms he resisted the assumption that we can get closer to the truth by abandoning metaphor. Because we grapple with a truth that is beyond our understanding, we must rely on the poetic imagination, not "the crumbling of texts."

In this context, while Thomas did not publish any poems that are about the Scriptures in the same way as Herbert's "H. Scriptures," he wrote two striking poems about William Morgan, who translated the Bible into Welsh in the late sixteenth century. The first, "Llanrhaeadr ym Mochnant" from *Not That He Brought Flowers* (1968), concludes:

> The smooth words
> Over which his mind flowed
> Have become an heirloom. Beauty
> Is how you say it, and the truth,
> Like this mountain-born torrent,
> Is content to hurry
> Not too furiously by.

The second, "R.I.P 1588–1988" from *Mass for Hard Times* (1992), is long (ninety-five lines) compared with the vast majority of his poems. It contains similar celebratory words about the beauties of Morgan's language and its place in Welsh culture and faith, combined with a sharp critique of the desiccating assumptions of contemporary society. Here Thomas noted, "Language can be / like iron. Are we sure we can bend / the Absolute to our meaning?" His conclusion we may take as his comment on the consequences of biblical criticism based on the model of scientific rationalism:

> In the beginning
> was the word. What
> word? At the end
> is the dust. We know
> what dust; the dust
> that the bone comes to,
> that is the fall-out
> from our hubris, the
> dust on the Book
> that, out of breath
> with our hurry
> we dare not blow off
> in a cloud, lest out
> of that cloud should

be resurrected the one
spoken figure we have grown
too clever to believe in.

Generally, however, his references are not to a document, a book, but to the Gospel or the Word, which have a more evocative quality, reflecting his consciousness of the poetic power of the stories the Scriptures tell and their allusive richness.

In "Gospel Truth" from the collection *Pieta* (1966) the allusions, at first, seem remote. In form the poem is a series of eleven sestets each ascribed to a member of a rural family (the Puws), father, mother and two sons. The pattern is for each of the sons to speak, then the father, then the mother, but in the third repetition there are only three voices, the father is absent. "There is," one son says, "an empty / Place at the table." The tone emphasizes the hardness of life in rural Wales. The title, then, seems only an invocation of the colloquial expression used to affirm the veracity of something, as if the poet were saying this is the gospel truth about trying to eke out a living from the land. But what it means for something to be "the gospel truth" depends on whether one believes that the Gospel is true. If one does not, then the phrase is ironic. Unless, of course, one uses the term without regard for its origins. That is unlikely for a poet, especially for a poet who was also a priest.

Two other aspects of the poem suggest the studied use of the title. The father of the family is Luke, the mother is Mair (Mary) and the sons Matthew and Mark. The choice is hardly coincidental, yet we need to tread carefully here: we cannot separate out the voices and say this one is distinctly Marcan, that one Matthean. The poetic instinct here is allusive, not literal. The second aspect to note is the persistent sense of an absence that is like a presence, the sense of someone distinctly other that suffuses the bleakly quotidian life of the family.

In contrast, "Gospel" directs the power of allusion to a broader stage than rural Wales:

> And in the midst of the council
> a bittern called from the fen
> outside. A sparrow flew in
> and disappeared through the far doorway.
> 'If your faith can explain...' So
> they were baptised, and the battles began
> for the kingdom of this world. Were
> you sent, sparrow? An eagle

would have been more appropriate,
some predator to warn them
of the ferocity of the religion
that came their way. The fire was not more voluble
than the blood that would answer the sword's
question.
                    Charles by divine right
king. And not all our engines can drain
Marston Moor. The bittern
is silent now. The ploughshares are beaten
to guns and bombs. Daily we publish
hurrying with it to and fro on steel
wings, the good news of the kingdom.
                    —*Later Poems, 1972–1982*

The irony here is so hard-edged that we wonder whether it is simply sarcasm. From the reference to the council that led to the conversion of the Saxon king to the failures of a "divine right" king, the claims of the Gospel are subdued to the demands of purely worldly sovereignties. And while the reference is not specific the lines "The ploughshares are beaten / to guns and bombs" chastises modern society through a striking reversal of the biblical cry for peace. A number of Thomas's poems are like scorpions with a powerful sting in the tail, the concluding lines. "Gospel" illustrates this well. The phrase, "the good news of the kingdom," hangs like a judgment over the sweep of history. Yet there is also ambiguity here. Is the judgment also against the failure of the Gospel, or at least those who hurry "to and fro on steel wings" proclaiming it? Or is there here an affirmation that despite all — all the wars, the deaths, the lust for power, the devastating weaponry — the good news persists, the telling of it goes on in boundless hope? Just as, even amid the timeless toil of the rural poor, the sense of a presence beyond continues its almost inaudible whisper.

We are struck again by the provisional quality of Thomas's individual poems: the fact that, while each stands very well by itself, each gains in resonance and meaning when read against earlier and later poems. Like "shards of brittle crazie glass," the individual poems interact with one another to form greater patterns — or to introduce a new perspective on a question or a new question about a tentative answer.

Thomas published two poems entitled "The Word." The first appeared in *Laboratories of the Spirit* (1975):

A pen appeared, and the god said:
'Write what it is to be
man.' And my hand hovered
long over the bare page,

until there, like footprints
of the lost traveller, letters
took shape on the page's
blankness, and I spelled out

the word 'lonely.' And my hand moved
to erase it; but the voices
of all those waiting at life's
window cried out loud: 'It is true.'

The poem seems not to be about the Scriptures at all, nor about the dealings of God with man, for how can The Word, the Good News, be reduced to "lonely"? The poet takes the pen, struggles until the word appears, not from his conscious intent, but from without. He merely traces the word already there. No, he thinks, and starts to erase it, but the voices compel him to halt. Is it true? "Those waiting at life's window" declare it so. But who are they? More importantly, are they outside looking in? or inside looking out? Is life within or without? What are they waiting for?

Waiting is a theme that returns again and again in Thomas's poetry and over the years he composed several poems with the title "Waiting." The first of them from *Frequencies* (1978) concludes: "waiting, / somewhere between faith and doubt, / for the echoes of its arrival." Here "its" refers to the name of God, to the word of God heard in our lives, and therefore by implication his presence. To assert the absence of God may mean to deny his existence, but that is never Thomas's point, as he showed in "The Presence" from his collection *Between Here and Now* (1981):

I pray and incur
silence. Some take that silence
for refusal.
            I feel the power
that, invisible, catches me
by the sleeve, nudging
            towards the long shelf

> that has the book on it I will take down
>   and read and find the antidote
> to an ailment.

The poem continues shifting from the notion of looking into a book to the notion of looking into a mirror, as if invoking Herbert's "the thankfull glass." (This is one of a number of poems in which Thomas uses a mirror as a device with at least an implied reference to the idea that we are made in the image of God.) When our experience of him is silence, however, we must wait.

> I know its ways with me;
> how it enters my life,
>   is present rather
> before I perceive it, sunlight quivering
> on a bare wall.

In waiting we may doubt, but we do not deny, for in waiting there is always expectation, always hope, that we will again hear. The hope may be frail, but in the rocky soil of our all-too-human faith, it persists with remarkable hardiness.

That hardiness finds full voice in the another of the poems entitled "Waiting":

> Here are mountains to ascend
> not to preach from,
> not to summon one's disciples
> to, but to see far off the dream that is life:
> winged yachts hovering over
> a gentian sea; sun-making
> windscreens; the human torrent
> irrigating tunefully the waste places.
>
> Ah, Jerusalem, Jerusalem!
> Is it for nothing our chapels were christened
> with Hebrew names? The Book rusts
> in the empty pulpits above empty
> pews, but the Word ticks inside
> remorselessly as the bomb that is timed soon to go off.
> —*Welsh Airs* (1987)

Herbert, writing within the ethos of seventeenth-century England when the King James Version of the Bible was fresh, could easily move from "this book of starres" to the Living Word. For Thomas, the distinction between the Book, this document of human language, and the Word, the divine truth that we struggle to articulate, made such movement difficult, if not impossible. In a much earlier poem, "A Welsh Testament" from *Tares* (1961), he spoke of trying to cram God "Between the boards of a black book." Yet the Word remains in all its force.

The waiting of "those at life's window" leads here, where, despite the emptiness of pulpit and pew, the Word still lives in all its transforming power. It leads also to the second poem entitled "The Word" (*Mass for Hard Times*, 1992):

> Enough that we are on our way;
> never ask of us where.
>
> Some of us run, some loiter;
> some of us turn aside
>
> to erect the Calvary
> that is our signpost, arms
>
> pointing in opposite directions
> to bring us in the end
>
> to the same place, so impossible
> is it to escape love. Imperishable
>
> scarecrow, recipient of out cast-offs,
> shame us until what is a swear-
>
> word only becomes at last
> the word that was in the beginning.

We are brought back, then, to the final lines of his second William Morgan poem, to "the one / spoken figure we have grown / too clever to believe in": Jesus, God's grandest metaphor, who was in the beginning, now is and evermore shall be.

3.

Having observed the ways the two poets invoked or commented upon the Scriptures in general, it may be instructive to examine how they approach a specific text. Herbert wrote five poems whose titles directly refer to specific passages in the Bible: "Coloss. iii. 3. Our life is hid with Christ in God," "Eph. iv. 30. Grieve not the Holy Spirit &c," "The Odour. 2Cor. ii. 15," "The 23d Psalme," and "The Pearl. Matt. xiii. 45." Not surprisingly in Thomas's work specific references are more allusive, though he too wrote poems whose titles made specific biblical references ("Hebrews 12:29" and "John 8"). And in "The Bright Field" (*Laboratories of the Spirit*), he used the same Matthean text ("Again the kingdom of heaven is like a merchant in search of fine pearls, who, on finding one pearl of great value, went and sold all that he had and bought it") and did so again in "The Pearl" (*No Truce with the Furies*).

Having inveighed against "crumbling a text into small parts," Herbert in his "The Pearl" remained true to that principle. (One can say the same about the other poems noted above.) He did not explicate the simile that the kingdom of heaven is like a pearl of great price. Rather, he accepted it and used it as a lodestar for commenting upon his own life. He began:

> I Know the wayes of Learning; both the head
> And pipes that feed the presse, and make it runne;
> What reason hath from nature borrowed,
> Or of it self, like a good huswife, spunne
> In laws and policie; what the starres conspire,
> What willing nature speaks, what forc'd by fire;
> Both th'old discoveries, and the new-found seas,
> The stock and surplus, cause and historie:
> All these stand open, or I have the keyes:
> > Yet I love thee.

The second and third stanzas follow the same form treating "the wayes of Honour" and "the wayes of Pleasure," detailing his intimacy with them and their appeal. Always he ended, "Yet I love thee." The fourth stanza asserts the consequences of that love, his choice to turn from the ways of the world to pursue the kingdom of heaven.

> I know all these, and have them in my hand:
> Therefore not sealed, but with open eyes

I flie to thee, and fully understand
Both the main sale, and the commodities;
With all the circumstances that may move:
And at what rate and price I have thy love;
Yet through these labyrinths, not my groveling wit,
But thy silk twist let down from heav'n to me,
Did both conduct and teach me, how by it
        To climbe to thee.

Taken as a whole the poem summarizes Herbert's life and affirms the consciousness of his choice, finally and in spite of his own qualms about his worthiness, to seek first the kingdom of heaven. Yet the final lines assert eloquently his understanding that it was the grace of God ("thy silk twist") which enabled him to give motion to the choice.

In "The Bright Field" Thomas used the "pearl of great price" as a gloss upon one of the moments of epiphany when he experienced a sense of God's elusive presence.

I have seen the sun break through
to illuminate a small field
for a while, and gone my way
and forgotten it. But that was the pearl
of great price, the one field that had
the treasure in it. I realize now
that I must give all that I have
to possess it. Life is not hurrying

on to a receding future, nor hankering after
an imagined past. It is the turning
aside like Moses to the miracle
of the lit bush, to a brightness
that seemed as transitory as your youth
once, but is the eternity that awaits you.

In contrast to this usage and to Herbert's, Thomas in "The Pearl," though also writing in the first person, did not set forth an epitome of his spiritual life. Neither did he resort to a mere explication of the text. The poem is in the form of a dialogue, bordering on a monologue with the dominant voice identifiable with the snake in the Garden of Eden. And it is that sibilant, satanic voice which invokes the Matthean reference in the final line.

'I think we have not,'
I said, 'been introduced.'

'No need,' it replied;
'I introduced myself

in the Garden, metallic
of scale, offering

the future to you in place
of the god's past. Would you

grow wings, anticipate
the clock? Behold, I am

at your door, in your
kitchen, at your bed's

side. I was the irritant
in the oyster that was

Leonardo's brain you have
split open to prove

to your conditioned audience
there is no pearl without price.'
                    — *No Truce with the Furies*

The devil quotes scripture to suit his purpose. But, of course, the quote is not entirely accurate (perhaps an echo of Satan tempting Jesus in the wilderness) and its imperfection recalls the original text and its context, the effort to describe the kingdom of heaven. A pearl has been bought with coin needed for the Pearl: the true cost of this lesser pearl, then, is the greater one. The final line thus has the ironic sting that characterizes many of Thomas's poems.

One may read this as a cranky old man inveighing against modernity, for it comes from Thomas's last collection, published in 1995. Yet, this is hardly a new theme in his poetry and we have long passed a time when the easy belief in the myth of human progress made sense, when we can regard all the fruits of human knowledge as beneficent. And nowhere in his poetry did Thomas suggest that the alternative choice is an easy one. He never proclaimed "Seek ye first the kingdom of heaven and everything will be fine." Indeed, in contrast to the familiar presence "at your door, in your / kitchen, at your bed's / side," the persistent silence of God is daunting. But, the choice remains.

4.

In a poem entitled "Resurrections," also from *No Truce with the Furies*, Thomas declared:

> Easier for them, God
> only at the beginning
> of his recession. Blandish him,
> said the times and they did so,
> Herbert, Traherne, walking
> in a garden not yet
> polluted....

We can hardly overestimate the intellectual and cultural gulf between the worlds which Herbert and Thomas inhabit. Modern science, technological revolutions, political transformations, and, as noted in the beginning, post-Enlightenment biblical criticism, all "pollute" the garden of the contemporary poetic imagination. At the same time life in England in the early seventeenth century was certainly not Edenic, even for someone of Herbert's connections. Indeed, those very connections made it impossible for him to be unaware of the religious and political controversies besetting England.

He chose to live the last few years of his life outside the vortex of those controversies, in a rural parish within a few miles of Salisbury Cathedral, but that life, if happy and productive in many respects, was hardly idyllic. By all accounts he was a caring and compassionate pastor to his people and the daily tasks of such service are burdens often unimaginable to those who have not borne them. And always there were the personal spiritual struggles to which his poetry is an enduring testament. In those struggles "this book of starres" was an abiding force. But, as noted earlier, as a classicist and a poet he knew the limits of language and the approximate quality of metaphor and simile.

For Thomas, God was more distant, or at least more often silent. Like Herbert, he addressed God directly in his poems, but, amidst the static of contemporary life, he seldom heard the answers—if there are any. The Bible could not be for him the unequivocal Word of God. Yet, for all that, he continued to struggle Jacob-like with the central question of Christianity, the Incarnate Word. It is a struggle he eloquently describes in "The Combat" from *Laboratories of the Spirit*:

> You have no name.
> We have wrestled with you all
> day, and now night approaches,
> the darkness from which we emerged
> seeking; and anonymous
> you withdraw, leaving us nursing
> our bruises, our dislocations.
>
> For the failure of language
> there is no redress. The physicists
> tell us your size, the chemists
> the ingredients of your
> thinking. But who you are
> does not appear, nor why
> on the innocent marches
> of vocabulary you should choose
> to engage us, belabouring us
> with your silence. We die, we die
> with the knowledge that your resistance
> is endless at the frontier of the great poem.

As C. S. Lewis observed, "The very essence of our life as conscious beings, all day and every day, consists of something which cannot be communicated except by hints, similes, metaphors, and the use of those emotions (themselves not very important) which are pointers to it" ("The Language of Religion," *Christian Reflections*, p. 140). Both Thomas and Herbert were poets, priests, pilgrims. For both, words were what they had to plumb the depths, to seek and express the meaning for themselves and others of the Word.

IV

Speaking to God: Prayer

In the late 1960s Thomas edited a selection of Herbert's poems, *A Choice of George Herbert's Verse* (London, 1967). It is an abundant choice representing somewhat more than forty percent of the contents of *The Temple*. While selective, Thomas essentially left those he used in Herbert's order. Thomas stated, somewhat cryptically, in an editor's note, "I have chosen mainly those poems which seem to me satisfactory as such." In his introduction, he observed that Herbert "demonstrates both the possibility and the desirability of a friendship with God. Friendship is no longer the right way to describe it. The word now is dialogue, encounter, confrontation, but the realities engaged have not altered all that much" (p. 16). Late in his life, however, Thomas remarked that he had "lost the ability to read Herbert," saying "I cannot get on 'matey' terms with the Deity as Herbert can" (RST personal interview with John McEllhenney, November 10, 1994). Both of these statements touch the manner of address to God and, almost by definition therefore, deal with prayer.

Prayer has two aspects: one as part of corporate worship and the other as an expression of personal devotion. As rural parish priests, Herbert and Thomas presided at public services within worshipping communities for whom common prayer was central. Both, also, recognized individual prayer as an essential part of the discipline of their lives as priests. Not surprisingly, therefore, the act of prayer, the substance of prayer, and the efficacy of prayer are themes that find expression in their poetry.

1.

In *A Country Parson*, Herbert spoke directly to the centrality of prayer in the life of the church and of the responsibility of the priest to set the example of proper reverence:

> The Country Parson, when he is to read divine services, composeth himself to all possible reverence; lifting up his heart and hands, and eyes, and using all other gestures which may expresse a hearty, and unfeyned devotion. This he doth, first, as being truly touched and amazed with the Majesty of God, before whom he then presents himself; yet not as himself alone, but as presenting with himself the whole Congregation, whose sins he then beares, and brings with his own to the heavenly altar to be bathed, and washed in the sacred Laver of Christs blood. Secondly, as this is the true reason of his inward feare, so he is content to expresse this outwardly to the utmost of his power; that being first affected himself, hee may affect also his people, knowing that no Sermon moves them so much to a reverence ... when they come to pray, as a devout behaviour in the very act of praying [Ch. 5].

Herbert proceeded to describe in detail the manner in which the priest should pray and the congregation respond. His description is a classic statement of Anglican seemliness and might draw comment for an apparent preoccupation with form. Yet a careful reading of Herbert leaves no doubt that what he sought was an outward and visible sign of a real, an unfeigned, devotion. Certainly his focus on appearance derived from his sense of responsibility for the spiritual health of the congregation.

The same can be said for his obvious interest in church architecture. His first ecclesiastical appointment was as canon and prebend for St. Mary's, Leighton Bromswold in Huntingdonshire (near Little Gidding). This was a non-parochial appointment, but Herbert oversaw the rebuilding of the church. One of the notable features of the restored church for which Herbert was particularly responsible is that the pulpit and the reading desk are identical in height and pattern in accordance with his conviction that prayer and preaching should be equally regarded. Indeed, in the "architecture" of his collected poems he began with a long series of verses entitled "The Church-porch" which includes the following lines: "Resort to sermons, but to prayers most: / Praying's the end of preaching."

In a church still struggling over questions of both doctrine and form, Herbert stood clearly with the view expressed by Richard Hooker. In the fifth book of his *The Laws of Ecclesiastical Polity*, Hooker not only defined the nature of prayer and its appropriate content, he also affirmed the primacy of corporate prayer. In a particularly telling and eloquent passage, Hooker writes:

> Between the throne of God in heaven and his Church upon earth here militant if it be so that Angels have their continual intercourse, where should we find the same more verified than in these two ghostly exercises, the one Doctrine, the other Prayer? For what

is the assembling of the Church to learn, but the receiving of Angels descended from above? What to pray, but the sending of Angels upward? His heavenly inspirations and our holy desires are as so many Angels of intercourse and commerce between God and us. As teaching bringeth us to know that God is our supreme truth; so prayer testifieth that we acknowledge him our sovereign good [Bk. V, ch. xxiii].

Herbert's own remarks quoted above seem merely a gloss on those of Hooker. As eloquent as Hooker was, however, Herbert went him one further. In "The Church-porch" he wrote

> Though private prayer be a brave designe,
> Yet publick hath more promises, more love:
> And love's a weight to hearts, to eies a signe.
> We all are cold but suitours; let us move
>   Where it is warmest. Leave thy six and seven
>   Pray with the most: for where most pray is heaven.
> —ll. 397–402

And, in the first of his two poems entitled "Prayer," Herbert's poetic eloquence soars:

> Prayer the Churches banquet, Angels Age
>   Gods breath in man returning to his birth,
>   The soul in paraphrase, heart in pilgrimage,
> The Christian plummet sounding heav'n and earth;
> Engine against th' Almightie, sinners towre,
>   Reversed thunder, Christ-side-piercing spear,
>   The six daies world transposing in an houre,
> A kinde of tune, which all things heare and fear;
> Softnesse, and peace, and joy, and love, and blisse,
>   Exalted Manna, gladnesse of the best,
>   Heaven in ordinarie, man well drest,
> The milkie way, the birde of Paradise,
>   Church-bels beyond the starres heard, the souls bloud,
>   The land of spice; something understood.

In this rhapsodic medley of images and metaphors, Herbert captured all that he understood of the act, the substance, and the efficacy of prayer, especially the prayer of the Church. It is a hymn to common prayer. The prayer of the church assembled is praise and thanksgiving and a means of aligning our wills with God's. The prayer of petition should express our "holy desires," not just our wants. It is precisely because common prayer raises the eyes of the individual beyond selfish desires that Herbert found it preferable. Here again we recognize that for Herbert the spiritual life was not solely interior, but required community as well. Neither Herbert nor Thomas, however, would assert that common prayer always rises above human selfishness.

As we have seen Thomas penned no such document as *A Priest to the Temple,* nor do we find in his works a poem equivalent to "Prayer (I)." Yet, here and there, we encounter at least the echoes of the convictions that underlay Hooker's argument and Herbert's poesy.

There is also an echo in Thomas's own recurrent concern with the architecture and décor of the churches that he served. Unlike Herbert, he was not into renovation, though both in Eglwys Fach and Aberdaron, he had his wife design wrought iron chandeliers for the sanctuary. He sensed the effects of such things on worship. While he clearly preferred simplicity, it is aesthetically pleasing simplicity. In his poems, however, his descriptions of churches tend to emphasize their spareness, their quiet, and at times their coldness, and not often did he describe the people at prayer. Yet, in "The Chapel," he told of a country church "becalmed in a last-century greyness" where

> ... once on an evening like this,
> in the darkness that was about
> his hearers, a preacher caught fire
> and burned steadily before them
> with a strange light, so that they saw
> the splendour of the barren mountains
> about them and sang their amens
> fiercely, narrow but saved
> in a way that men are not now.
> — *Laboratories of the Spirit* (1975)

A striking early poem, "Maes-yr-Onnen," describes a small nonconformist chapel that was always a favorite of his:

> Though I describe it stone by stone, the chapel
> Left stranded in the hurrying grass,
> Painting faithfully the mossed tiles and the tree,
> The one listener to the long homily
> Of the ministering wind, and the dry, locked doors,

The main altar of St. Hywyn's. Thomas and his wife designed the chandelier.

And the stale piety, mouldering within;
You cannot share with me that rarer air,
Blue as a flower and heady with the scent
Of the years past and others yet to be,
That brushed each window and outsoared the clouds'
Far foliage with its own high canopy.
You cannot hear as I, incredulous, heard
Up in the rafters, where the bell should ring,
The wild, sweet singing of Rhiannon's birds.
                            — *An Acre of Land* (1952)

Another echo reverberates in his attitude toward the liturgical changes that characterized the church in the last years of his ministry. In *The Echoes Return* he wryly remarked, "Revision was in the air. Language was out of date; too formal. God was available for conversation. Bishops were overawed by the theologians. What committee ever composed a poem?" (p. 96). At one point he agreed to serve on a liturgical committee of the Church in Wales. After one meeting he sent a postcard resigning. More strikingly and powerfully he begins the long poem "Bleak Liturgies" thusly:

Shall we revise the language?
And in revising the language
will we alter the doctrine?

Do we seek to plug the hole
in faith with faith's substitute
grammar? And are we to be saved

by translation? As one by one
the witnesses died off
they commended their metaphors

to our notice. For two thousand
years the simplistic recipients
of the message pointed towards

the reductionist solution. We devise
an idiom more compatible with
the furniture departments of our churches.
                    — *Mass for Hard Times* (1992)

It would be easy enough to dismiss these words as the waspish plaint of a traditionalist clinging to the old language, but a full reading of Thomas suggests far more. They are also the words of a poet who profoundly understood the nature and value of metaphorical language — and of a Christian who believed that the dark hard rocks of the faith can only be expressed in metaphors. And metaphor speaks to our understanding suggestively, impressionistically, never definitively. Thus our understanding remains imperfect. If we in our contemporary wisdom (or is it arrogance?) decry "the reductionist solution" of the past, can we really believe that our own flight from metaphor, the conviction that we can precisely state religious truths in "furniture department" language, is not also reductionist? Does our "fraction of the language" really lead us anywhere in our journey of faith? "Is / to grow up to destroy / childhood's painting of one / who was nothing but vocabulary's / shadow?" ("Bleak Liturgies").

Thomas wrote also as one who had experienced the dailiness of rural parish life, tending to the cares and concerns and spiritual needs of people largely unacquainted with the conversations in church administrative centers and university theology departments. And for those people he recognized the value of communal worship, of common prayer, "to escape from the echo of their silence." And they escape from that silence by hearing again, by reciting again, the familiar words of scripture and liturgy. The most telling argument for liturgical revision is to bring people closer to worship. But it is also true that unfamiliar words alienate people, render opaque the "soul windows" which familiar words and texts create. (See John McEllhenney, "R. S. Thomas: Poet for Turn-of-the-Millenium Believers," *Quarterly Review* [Fall 1999], pp. 267–292, esp. 282–285.)

In time, of course, the new words, the new prayers, become familiar and may have the same vital force as the old words and prayers (leaving aside the question of the quality of the new language itself). But for some people that will never happen: for most people there is a time after which learning a "new language" is no longer possible, at least in the sense of acquiring real facility and ease. Is it a sufficient answer in such a matter to say that, while the loss such people may suffer is regrettable, it is necessary? And even if the answer to the question now is yes, can that answer suffice time and again? As is already evident, the same argument that justified the changes that Thomas responded to impels another and yet another round of revision. "Do we seek to plug the hole / in faith with faith's substitute / grammar? And are we to be saved / by translation?"

Again, in his introduction to Herbert, Thomas stated, "To him Anglicanism was a way of life. It was a commitment to an order of reason, discipline and propriety, embodied in a Church solidly based on Scripture and the Book of Common Prayer. Is this deliberate submission to such a wholesome way of life entirely without relevance or appeal at the present time?" (p. 16). Following his retirement from the active ministry in 1978, Thomas long continued to take services in some of the tiny chapels scattered throughout the area. According to John McEllhenney one of the reasons he did so was that he regarded the Eucharist as central to common worship and therefore wanted to be sure that the people who faithfully attended those places could receive the sacrament. And he continued to participate in the corporate worship of the church. Seemingly then, Thomas found Herbert's example relevant and consistent with his own practice. Thus, in regard to the matter of public prayer, the prayer of the church, Thomas, too, reflects the Anglican tradition that Hooker defined so aptly, and which Herbert called "the Churches banquete."

2.

It is in the context of personal prayer that Thomas's sense of alienation from Herbert seems most vivid.

Regarded as a "picture of the many spiritual conflicts which have passed betwixt God and my soul," Herbert's poetry shows him struggling with doubts about his own worthiness and with anxieties produced by a recurrent sense of the silence of God. However, the overall impression he presented was, that for all his weakness and deficiencies, God had used him, and that God's silence never betokened absence. The closing phrase of his commission to Ferrar to do what he thought best with the poems says it well, "I have now found perfect freedom." One of the means by which he achieved that freedom was prayer.

Regarded less personally as a description of the Christian spiritual life (albeit one informed by his own experience), *The Temple* still illustrates the centrality of prayer, both corporate and individual, to that life. Prayer is the exercise by which the individual sustains himself through those periods of doubt, of despair, over one's own weaknesses and the silences of God.

In *A Country Parson* Herbert affirmed the role of prayer in the life of a priest: prayer before the study of Scripture, prayer before eating, prayer before worship, prayer before preaching. Indeed, many of his poems have the form of prayers: prayers of praise, of petition, of thanksgiving. It is undoubtedly the tone of these prayer-poems to which Thomas referred when he says, "I cannot get on 'matey' terms with the Deity as Herbert can." That is perhaps unfair to Herbert, who is too "touched and amazed with the Majesty of God" ever to address God as a chum. Still, it is the apparent ease of Herbert's sure and certain hope of being answered that was the source of Thomas's discomfort. That would certainly explain the omission from his selection of Herbert's "Prayer (II)"—though one may assume he also had poetic reasons.

> Of what an easie quick accesse,
> My blessed Lord, art thou! how suddenly
>   May our requests thine eare invade!
> To shew that state dislikes not easinesse,
> If I but lift mine eyes, my suit is made:
> Thou canst no more not heare, than thou canst die.
>
> Of what supreme almightie power
> Is thy great arm, which spans the east and west,
>   And tacks the centre to the sphere!
> By it do all things live their measur'd houre:
> We cannot ask the thing, which is not there,
> Blaming the shallowness of our request.
>
> Of what unmeasurable love
> Art thou possest, who, when thou couldst not die,

Wert fain to take our flesh and curse,
And for our sakes in person sinne reprove,
That by destroying that which ty'd thy purse,
Thou mightst make way for liberalitie!

  Since then these three wait on thy throne,
Ease, Power, and *Love*; I value prayer so,
    That were I to leave all but one,
Wealth, fame, endowments, vertues, all should go;
I and deare prayer would together dwell,
And quickly gain, for each inch lost, an ell.

Certainly here is a paean to the efficacy of prayer. Herbert, however, was not arguing that whatever we might pray for, we will receive. With Hooker, Herbert recognized that the great danger of private, as opposed to communal prayer, is that of ourselves we are more likely to ask selfish things. We need to be careful, he would say, that our prayers of petition reflect holy desires. In any case, as the first of the many proverbs Herbert listed in his *Jacula Prudentum* states, "Man proposeth, God disposeth." And, after all, God knows what we will ask even before we pray, so why bother? With Hooker, Herbert would reply "Prayer testifieth that we acknowledge him our sovereign good." With Augustine, Herbert would say, "Thou art never far from us, though we be far from Thee." Prayer is ultimately a duty and discipline, a means, perhaps the most important means we have, of aligning our will with God's, of knowing his presence.

As suggested earlier, I think "friendship" is not quite the right word to use in describing Herbert's sense of relationship with God. His mode of address is consistently deferential and reverential: "My God and King," "My Lord," "My Master." Indeed, with the exception of the poem "Jesu," even his references to Jesus are always as "My Lord," "My Saviour" or "Christ." Here Herbert's attitude is consistent with that which John Wesley later expressed in his sermon "On Knowing Christ after the Flesh":

> From the time that we are created anew in Christ Jesus we do not think, or speak, or act, with regard to our blessed Lord, as a mere man. We do not now use any expression with relation to Christ which may not be applied to him not only as he is man, but as he is "God over all, blessed for ever."

Thus, even for Herbert, "dialogue" and "encounter" are much more apt. Whatever one calls it, however, the dominant quality in his sense of the relationship is the pervasive conviction of the presence of God (even when we know it not), the responsiveness of God (even in his silences), and the love of God.

If Herbert was closer to Thomas than the latter's comments made later in life would suggest, it is nonetheless true that Thomas could never say with Herbert, "Of what an easie quick accesse / My blessed Lord, art thou!" Perhaps indicative of the beginning of Thomas's loss of comfort with Herbert is the opening poem of *Laboratories of the Spirit* (1975):

> Not as in the old days I pray,
> God. My life is not what it was.
> Yours, too, accepts the presence of
> the machine? Once I would have asked
> healing. I go now to be doctored,
> to drink sinlessly of the blood
> of my brother, to lend my flesh
> as manuscript of the great poem
> of the scalpel. I would have knelt
> long, wrestling with you, wearing
> you down. Hear my prayer, Lord, hear
> my prayer. As though you were deaf, myriads
> of mortals have kept up their shrill
> cry, explaining your silence by
> their unfitness.
>   It begins to appear
> This is not what prayer is about.
> It is the annihilation of difference,
> the consciousness of myself in you,
> of you in me; the emerging
> from the adolescence of nature
> into the adult geometry
> of the mind. I begin to recognize
> you anew, God of form and number.
> There are questions we are the solution
> to, others whose echoes we must expand
> to contain. Circular as our way
> is, it leads not back to that snake-haunted
> garden, but onward to the tall city
> of glass that is the laboratory of the spirit.
>   —"Emerging"

The title of the collection itself suggests the quality of testing, of seeking. This quality is not new to Thomas, but from this point on it seemed more central, more urgent, as the titles of subsequent collections reflect: *Frequencies* (1978), *Between Here and Now* (1981), *Destinations* (1985), and *Experimenting with an Amen* (1986). Individually, each of these collections reflects the tentative character of Thomas's work as he turned ideas, images, metaphors, this way and that. He strives, not for one definitive view of truth, but for an accumulation of perspectives that will bring us closer to understanding.

"Emerging" announces a movement away from the prayer of petition, the kind of prayer about which the first three stanzas of Herbert's "Prayer (II)" appear to speak. Instead, it describes prayer as "the annihilation of difference, the consciousness of myself in you, of you in me." Yet, how different is this from Herbert's concluding stanza in which he eschewed "wealth, fame, endowments, vertues"—the kinds of things we so often pray for in prayers of petition—for prayer itself as the act of aligning the self with the will of God? That is a distinct theme in Anglican theology. In his *Participation in God: A Forgotten Strand in Anglican Tradition*, A. M. Allchin identifies Hooker, Lancelot Andrewes, Charles and John Wesley, John Keble and E. B. Pusey among others as reflecting that theme. And in Herbert we find it as well:

> Christ is my onely head
> My alone onely heart and breast,
> My onely musick, striking me ev'n dead;
> That to the old man I may rest,
> And be in him new drest.
> *Aaron*

Also in *Laboratories of the Spirit*, Thomas wrote:

> He kneeled down
>   dismissing his orisons
> as inappropriate; one by one
>   they came to his lips and were swallowed
> but without bile.
>   He fell back
> on an old prayer: Teach me to know
>   what to pray for....

He listened and heard nothing but the "casualties / of his past intercessions." His mouth was dry.

... But the prayer formed:
Deliver me from the long drought
of the mind. Let leaves
from the deciduous Cross
fall on us, washing
us clean, turning our autumn
to gold by the affluence of their fountain.
—"The Prayer"

This poem is characteristic of Thomas in several ways. On the one
hand it is a reworking and refining of a much earlier poem "In a Country
Church" from *Song at the Year's Turning* (1955).

To one kneeling down no word came,
Only the wind's song, saddening the lips
Of the grave saints, rigid in glass;
Or the dry whisper of unseen wings,
Bats not angels, in the high roof.

Was he balked by silence? He kneeled long
And saw love in a dark crown
Of thorns blazing, and a winter tree
Golden with fruit of a man's body.

It also resembles, even relates to, other poems describing rural churches,
abandoned or empty, in which the "narrator" finds himself alone, struggling to pray.

... Why, then, do I kneel still
striking my prayers on a stone
heart? Is it in hope one
of them will ignite yet and throw
on its illumined walls the shadow
of someone greater than I can understand?
—"The Empty Church," *Frequencies* (1978)

The silence he encounters is both his own failure to find words and the
absence of any still small voice from God. Yet answers come, wordlessly perhaps, in sounds, in images, in some ineffable sense, in the persistence of questions that will not go away. Recall again the tenderness of his memory of
Maes-yr-Onnen. And always, among the shadows, the shadow of the Cross.

Thomas was an eloquent poet of God's silence, even of His absence, but absence is not nonexistence. In a poem "The Presence" from *Between Here and Now* (1981), he said:

> I pray and incur
> silence. Some take that silence
> for refusal.
>   I feel the power
> that, invisible, catches me
> by the sleeve, nudging
>   towards the long shelf
> that has the book on it I will take down
>   and read and find the antidote
> to an ailment.
>   I know its ways with me;
> how it enters my life,
>   is present rather
> before I perceive it, sunlight quivering
> on a bare wall.
>   Is it consciousness trying
> to get through?
>   Am I under
> regard?
>   It takes me seconds
> to focus, by which time
>   it has shifted its gaze,
> looking a little to one
>   side, as though I were not here.
>
> It has the universe
>   to be abroad in.
> There is nothing I can do
> but fill myself with my own
>   silence, hoping it will approach
>   like a wild creature to drink
> there, or perhaps like Narcissus
> to linger a moment over its transparent face.

This is a tenuous presence, seemingly momentary, almost incidental. We have the impersonal "it." How even does one pray to such a being? Only by silence? Yet hope persists, however tenuous. The closing lines allude to the idea that we are made in the image of God and so reopen the question of the personality of this impersonal being.

In a poem reflecting on Kierkegaard ("S. K.," *No Truce with the Furies*) Thomas concluded:

> Is prayer
> not a glass that, beginning
> in obscurity as his books
> do, the longer we stare
> into the clearer becomes
> the reflection of a countenance
> in it other than our own?

No "easie, quick accesse" here, yet reason enough to pray, to pray unceasingly.

> There are nights that are so still
> that I can hear the small owl calling
> far off and a fox barking
> miles away. It is then that I lie
> in the lean hours awake listening
> to the swell born somewhere in the Atlantic
> rising and falling, rising and falling
> wave on wave on the long shore
> by the village, that is without light
> and companionless. And the thought comes
> of that other being who is awake, too,
> letting our prayers break on him,
> not like this for a few hours,
> but for days, years, for eternity.
> —"The Other," *Destinations*

3.

Thomas observed, "Yeats said that out of his quarrel with others man makes rhetoric, but out of his quarrel with himself poetry. Herbert surely had no quarrel with others. What he had was an argument, not with others, not with himself primarily, but with God; and God always won" (*A Selection*, p. 12). Thomas seems more querulous, and he did not always resist arguing with others in verse, but, like Herbert, he argued more often with himself and most often with God — though it is not always clear with which of the two the argument is. It is precisely because prayer did not provide for Thomas "an easie quick accesse" that he argued and his commitment to that work was a driving force of his creativity. His persistence brings to mine C. S. Lewis's observation in the closing paragraph of *The Four Loves*: "If we cannot 'practice the presence of God', it is something to practice the absence of God, to become increasingly aware of our unawareness…" (p. 160).

No matter how far and wide our reading of Thomas is, we will not find the abundant sense of God's presence, the ease of address, which characterizes such Herbert poems as "Love (III)" — thus no buoyant "Love bade me welcome." For all the moments of crashing silence, of frayed hope, however, there are other moments, fragile and delicate, yet full of grace, such as that described in "The Answer" (*Frequencies*):

> … There have been times
> when, after long on my knees
> in a cold chancel, a stone has rolled
> from my mind, and I have looked
> in and seen the old questions lie
> folded and in a place
> by themselves, like the piled
> graveclothes of love's risen body.

V

The Bread of Truth: The Eucharist

As priests both Herbert and Thomas bore responsibility for leading liturgical worship. As stated in the previous chapter, they recognized that the common prayer of the worshiping community was essential to the Christian life. For both the central act of that community was the Eucharist. Herbert's vivid metaphor of prayer as "the Churches banquet" gives voice to this conviction, for it connects prayer and the eucharistic feast. Thomas provided no equivalent metaphor, but his readiness to continue supply work after his retirement in order that small parishes of rural Wales might have regular communion gave substance to the same conviction. For both, as well, the imagery of the eucharistic elements, the bread and wine, appears vividly in their poetry.

1.

Herbert lived in an era when the "Sacrament of the Lord's Supper" was a central issue of contention. Horton Davies has articulated the issue as follows:

> ... Was the Sacrament, as most Catholics and Anglicans believed, a means of grace, or, as many Puritans affirmed, was it mainly a mnemonic? That is, did the sacraments act as channels of grace that fortified the Christian soul (as bread and wine strengthen the body), or were they merely vivid reminders of the Cross and Resurrection of Jesus Christ and the benefits these events had brought to the faithful in the assurance of forgiveness and the promise of eternal life? [*Worship and Theology in England: IV From Andrewes to Baxter and Fox, 1603–1690*, p. 286].

Herbert was no controversialist, but he stood squarely with the former view, which is to say he held to the position affirmed in Article XXVIII of the Thirty-Nine Articles:

> The Supper of the Lord is not only a sign of the love that Christians ought to have among themselves one to another; but rather it is a Sacrament of our Redemption by Christ's death: insomuch that to such as rightly, worthily, and with faith, receive the same, the Bread which we break is a partaking of the Body of Christ; and likewise the Cup of Blessing is a partaking of the Blood of Christ.

In *The Country Parson*, he offered certain practical suggestions that illustrate the importance he attached to the Lord's Supper. He recommended that the parson celebrate communion once a month, but at the very least five or six times a year, and that everyone should receive no less than three times a year. (Judged by contemporary Anglican practice this may seem infrequent, but in the context of the seventeenth century, it affirms the importance of the sacramental life.) He also commented:

> The time of every ones first receiving is not so much by years, as by understanding: particularly, the rule may be this: When any one can distinguish the Sacramentall from the common bread, knowing the Institution, and the difference, hee ought to receive, of what age soever. Children and youths are usually deferred too long, under pretence of devotion to the Sacrament, but it is for want of Instruction; their understandings being ripe enough for ill things, and why not then for better? [*The Country Parson*, pp. 258–259].

The elements should be received kneeling, for while the sense of a feast suggests sitting, man's ill preparation for so great a gift begs kneeling. And finally Herbert insisted on the necessity of both priest and people approaching the sacrament with the thought and care so great a gift requires.

For Herbert the Lord's Supper represented the fountain of grace, the way to salvation. It is through the Eucharist that the Divine Love sheds its grace on man. In his poetry he frequently referred to the wound in Christ's side as "the open door" (e.g., "The Bag"), and this door he then identified with the communion service: "On Sunday heavens gate stands open." ("Sunday"). The celebration of the Lord's Supper is the happiest, yet the most burdensome, moment for the priest. In it he is called "not only to receive God, but to break, and administer Him." This awesome responsibility Herbert emphasized in "The Priesthood":

> But th'holy men of God such vessels are,
> As serve him up, who all the world commands:

When God vouchsafeth to become our fare,
Their hands convey him, who conveys their hands.
O what pure things, most pure must those things be,
    Who bring my God to me!

Herbert's acceptance of the real presence was both vigorous and graphic. Throughout his poetry he conveyed this conviction. In "The Banquet" he wrote, "Having rais'd me to look up, / In a cup / Sweetly he doth meet my taste." And in "The Agonie," he declared, "Love is that liquor sweet and most divine, / Which my God feels as bloud; but I, as wine." These are only two of many examples that illustrate his acknowledgment of the real presence. Of course, in the seventeenth century the question of the mode of that presence was also at issue. He showed little interest in that combative question, for to him the mode in no way changes the actuality of Christ's presence, nor the efficacy of that presence for the believer. In one of his two poems entitled "The Holy Communion" (note: the other, but not this one, is in the generally accepted manuscript of *The Temple*) he said:

O Gratious Lord, how shall I know
Whether in these gifts thou bee so
    As thou art evry-where;
Or rather so, as thou alone
Tak'st all the Lodging, leaving none
    ffor thy poore creature there?

ffirst I am sure, whether bread stay
Or whether Bread doe fly away
    Concerneth bread, not mee.
But that both thou and all thy traine
Bee there, to thy truth, & my gaine,
    Concerneth mee & Thee.

In the same poem, however, he went on to firmly reject (as do the Thirty-Nine Articles) the doctrine of transubstantiation: "Then of this also I am sure, / That thou didst all those pains endure / To' abolish Sinn, not Wheat."

It is also clear that he rejected the idea of receptionism, i.e. that it was the faith of the recipient that effected the real presence. He does not even appear to ascribe to Hooker's view which John Booty has described as "a doctrine of the real partaking of the body and blood of Christ in the

Eucharist, rather than a doctrine of the real presence of Christ in the Eucharist" (*The Spirit of Anglicanism*, p. 309). The awe in which he held the priestly office and the manner in which he described the priestly function suggest the intermediary role that the priest fulfills. In "The Invitation" he asserted, "Weep what ye have drunk amisse, / And drink this, / Which before ye drink is bloud." He made no effort, however, to go further and define the mode of the real presence. God himself provides no specific response and the speculations of men have only produced needless anguish. It is enough to know that God is there.

Herbert did affirm the theological understanding of the Lord's Supper as articulated in the Thirty-Nine Articles, that it is the "Sacrament of our Redemption by Christ's death." This is vividly expressed in his use of the image of the wound in Christ's side as the open door. It was the wound and the agony of Christ's death, not simply the Last Supper, that instituted the Sacrament: "Nay, after death their spite shall further go; / For they will pierce my side, I full well know; / That as sinn came, so Sacraments might flowe ..." ("The Sacrifice"). And in "The Agonie" he says "Who knows not Love, let him assay / And taste that juice, which on the crosse a pike / Did set again abroach...." In the poem "The H. Communion" from *The Temple* he declares:

> Onely thy grace, which with these elements comes,
>> Knoweth the readie way,
>> And hath the key,
> Op'ning the souls most subtile rooms....

And, "Thou hast restor'd us to this ease / By this thy heav'nly bloud...." Less explicit than such statements, but no less indicative of Herbert's eucharistic theology is his preoccupation with the Passion and Resurrection in all his poetry. His emphasis on the sacraments as the source of grace combined with the concreteness of his imagery furthers this impression.

Again, however, he was not concerned with dogmatic formulations. In his poetry, as in his preaching he chose "texts of Devotion, not Controversie." This may explain why he chose to omit the second "H. Communion" poem from his final arrangement of *The Temple*. His piety, to be sure, was intensely liturgical, even sacramental, in its expression — indeed it has its fullest expression in the Eucharist — but his primary concern was God's grace and man's salvation, and he preoccupied himself with the tasks of devotion. The fact that he regarded the Eucharist as a central task illustrates his conviction that the spiritual life is not solely interior, but also requires corporate activity. All this is evident in these stanzas from "The Banquet":

> O what sweetnesse from the bowl
>   Fills my soul,
> Such as is, and makes divine!
> Is some starre (fled from the sphere)
>   Melted there,
> as we sugar melt in wine?
>
> Or hath sweetnesse in the bread
>   Made a head
> To subdue the smell of sinne;
> Flowers, and gummes, and powders giving
>   All their living,
> Lest the enemy should winne?
>
> Doubtlesse, neither starre nor flower
>   Hath the power
> Such a sweetnesse to impart:
> Onely God, who gives perfumes,
>   Flesh assumes,
> And with it perfumes my heart.

2.

Thomas was no more interested in using his poetry to explore and articulate issues of eucharistic theology than was Herbert, indeed significantly less so. Obviously in the twentieth century the issues of the real presence and the mode of that presence were not matters of controversy as they had been in the seventeenth. On the other hand the years of Thomas's active ministry parallel a time when, within the Anglican communion, a conscious concern with the form and nature of the worship experience intensified, and historically that communion has regarded the Eucharist as the central rite of that experience. Thus, for him, as for Herbert, the Eucharist provided rich imagery. However, while Herbert, invoking that imagery, could assume it would evoke both theological and emotional particulars, for Thomas the imagery became more protean and more allusive, and as a result more surprising, perhaps for some readers more disturbing.

The earliest references in Thomas are tentative, ambiguous. The poem

"Absolution" from *Poetry for Supper* (1958) asks "can you forgive / From your stone altar on which the light's / Bread is broken at dusk and dawn...." He was describing the countryside and natural phenomena and asking his oft-named peasant, Prytherch, if he could forgive him his dismissive scorn. But the words "altar" and "bread" suggest the Eucharist and with it all its attendant connotations: the Sacrament as a channel of grace and inevitably the Cross.

In the same collection, the poem "Bread" brings to mind the notion of the "bread of life" and therefore again both sacrament and Cross:

> Hunger was loneliness, betrayed
> By the pitiless candour of the stars'
> Talk, in an old byre he prayed
>
> Not for food; to pray was to know
> Waking from a dark dream to find
> The white loaf on the white snow;
>
> Not for warmth, warmth brought the rain's
> Blurring of the essential point
> Of ice probing his raw pain.
>
> He prayed for love, love that would share
> His rags' secret; rising he broke
> Like sun crumbling the gold air
>
> The live bread for the starved folk.

Indeed we have here an evocation of the communion service itself.

In his early Christmas poems (see ch. XI) the reference is more specific as he describes parishioners in rural Wales wending their way to Christmas Eve services,

> ... there to kneel
> And eat the new bread
> Of love, washing it down
> With the sharp taste
> Of blood they will shed.
> —"Christmas," *Not That He Brought Flowers*

And

They came over the snow to the bread's
purer snow, fumbled it in their huge
hands, put their lips to it
like beasts, stared into the dark chalice
where the wine shone, felt it sharp
on their tongue, shivered as at a sin
remembered, and heard love cry
momentarily in their hearts' manger.
                    —"Hill Christmas," *Laboratories of the Spirit*

The second of these with its phrase "bread's purer snow" harks back to
"white loaf on the white snow" from "Bread" and therefore reiterates the
idea of the earlier poem being consciously eucharistic. As noted before,
Thomas often did this: his poems, even those separated by many years in
the composition, echo, comment upon, modify one another. The Christmas poems are not doctrinal poems, they are religious poems: that is, they
are attempts to describe metaphorically our experience with realities,
including our spiritual experience. And metaphor is always approximate,
and always capable of stimulating new insight.

   "Bread of life," "bread of love," and then in a subsequent collection,
The Bread of Truth (1963)—but here the meaning becomes even more
elusive. We find few ready evocations of the Eucharist, and the subject
matter itself seems to sprawl so that one wonders, "What is truth?" The
phrase itself appears in the poem "Servant" which is addressed to Prytherch, the recurrent figure of the rough, stolid Welsh peasant who appears
frequently in Thomas's early poems, but who, by this time, has become
only an occasional figure. The poet hails him saying, "You served me
well."

                    Not that you gave
The whole answer. Is truth so bare,
So dark, so dumb, as on your hearth
And in your company I found it?
Is not the evolving print of the sky
To be read, too; the mineral
Of the mind worked? Is not truth choice,
With a clear eye and a free hand,
From life's bounty?
                    Not choice for you,
But seed sown upon the thin
Soil of a heart, not rich, not fertile,

Yet capable of the one crop,
Which is the bread of truth that I break.

"The bread of truth that I break" clearly evokes the fraction at the Eucharist. In so doing Thomas suggested that the "one crop" which the heart of this prototypical Welsh peasant yields is linked to that truth of which the Eucharist is the outward and visible sign. This draws us back to the earlier images, bread of life and bread of love.

All those images echo again in the evocative poem in his next collection *Pieta* (1966), "The Moor," which ends: "I walked on, / Simple and poor, while the air crumbled / And broke on me generously as bread." Again and again we find this, an echo of earlier poems, a shadow of former words crossing over a new poem like a bird in flight, a vision of nature bound up with an image replete with religious meanings.

In his rural poems Thomas moved by fits and starts toward an admiration for the likes of Prytherch. He hardly idealized them or their lives; he authored no romantic pastorals. But he found in their steady endurance a virtue of simplicity that cannot be dismissed — at least not so easily as urbane moderns believe. That virtue allows them the experience of hearing love's cry which he so aptly described in "Hill Christmas" quoted earlier.

The collection from which that poem comes, *Laboratories of the Spirit*, contains nine other poems that explicitly invoke eucharistic images. In three of them the reference to the eucharistic elements is part of a powerful negative: "God / looking into a dry chalice, / felt the cold touch of the machine ..." ("God's Story"), "... And the spider would run / from the chalice, and the wine would lie / there for a time, cold and unwanted / by all but he ..." ("Post Restante"), "... wine poisoned / in the chalice ..." ("Thus"). The negative is not God's absence or silence, frequent themes in Thomas to be sure, but man's apostasy, his misplaced faith in technology. If one recalls the importance Thomas attached to the Eucharist as the central rite of community worship, then the dry or poisoned chalice and the unwanted wine manifest the failure of that center, the fracturing of that community.

In the other six poems, the references are more elliptical and more positive. One poem seems particularly rich and striking.

Suddenly

As I had always known
he would come, unannounced,

> remarkable merely for the absence
> of clamour. So truth must appear
> to the thinker; so, at a stage
> of the experiment, the answer
> must quietly emerge. I looked
> at him, not with the eye
> only, but with the whole
> of my being, overflowing with
> him as a chalice would
> with the sea. Yet was he
> no more there than before,
> his area occupied
> by the unhaloed presences.
> You could put your hand
> in him without consciousness
> of his wounds. The gamblers
> at the foot of the unnoticed
> cross went on with
> their dicing; yet the invisible
> garment for which they played
> was no longer at stake, but worn
> by him in this risen existence.

One could almost regard the allusion to the Eucharist as casual —
except there was never anything casual about Thomas's choice of words.
Inevitably "chalice" evokes the Eucharist and the use of the word at the
point where the poet writes of "the whole of my being, overflowing with
him" connects to the sense of God's presence (by whatever mode) in the
Sacrament. Thomas was not striving for any precise theological statement here, rather it is the openness of the metaphor and finally the ultimate mystery of God's presence that he articulated. It is that sense which
undergirded his valuing of the Eucharist. In the poem "Ann Griffith" he
wrote:

> ... These people know me
> only in the thin hymns of
> the mind, in the arid sermons
> and prayers. I am the live God,
> nailed fast to the old tree
> of a nation by its unreal
> tears. I thirst, I thirst

for the spring water. Draw it up
for me from your heart's well and I will change
it to wine upon your unkissed lips.

There is, of course, allusion to the marriage feast at Cana, but the invocation of the Crucifixion draws the remembrance of Jesus's wounded side,
Herbert's "open door" and thus inevitably of the Eucharist. (In "The
Prayer" Thomas said: "... He / held out his hands, cupped / as though to
receive blood, leaking / from life's side.") One can read this as a critique
of nonconformist worship and its overreliance on preaching and the con-
comitant devaluation of communion. And it is at least that, but Thomas's
purpose was more to celebrate Ann Griffith by suggesting she broke beyond
the aridity of that tradition to give voice to the "live God," in a sense as
one of the communion of saints.

One aspect of the Anglican emphasis on the Eucharist as the church's
central worship experience is the acceptance of it as a holy mystery. Herbert's acceptance of the Real Presence without defining the mode of that
presence is in that regard typically Anglican. Thomas's poem "Suddenly"
comes near to affirming God's presence at the altar, but not quite. Ultimately the elusiveness of God demonstrates the divine quality that Thomas
saw as most characteristic: he will come when he will come, not when we
will have him come. In that context the Eucharist appears to be a contra-
diction, for it is a human rite: if God is present every time we perform it
are we not controlling his presence? But what if we regard it not as an
action that calls God forth from somewhere distant to be here and now, it
is rather a prism or an amplifier which allows us to sense his presence? Its
mystery is finally its simplicity, a simplicity that lies beyond the limits of
chemical analysis or analytical philosophy.

Writing of his ministry at Aberdaron at the end of the Llyn Peninsula where the church stands overlooking the sea, Thomas says in *The
Echoes Return Slow*:

A bough of land between sea and sky with
the clouds for apple blossoms, white by day,
pink towards evening. This is where he had
crawled out, far as he could go, repeating the
pilgrimages of the saints. Had he like John
Synge come 'towards nightfall upon a race
passionate and simple like his heart'?
Simple certainly. There is an intellectual

The breaking of the wave
outside echoed the breaking
of the bread in his hands.

The crying of the sea gulls
was the cry from the Cross:
Lama Sabachthani. He lifted

snobbery. The simplicity of the Sacrament
absolved him from the complexities of the
Word.

the chalice, that crystal in
which love questioning is love
blinded with excess of light.

With this we come close to the source of Thomas's sometimes grudging, but always real, admiration for the people he served in rural Wales:
the recognition that they have an unassuming wisdom that exceeds eru-
dite knowledge. Their thirst for "the simplicity of the Sacrament" renders
moot learned expositions ("hymns of the mind" and "arid sermons"). To
digress momentarily, Allchin points out that the concluding image here
strongly echoes that of Dafydd ap Gwilym, the fourteenth-century Welsh
poet who spoke of "A chalice of ecstasy and love" (*God's Presence Makes
the World*, p. 156). Thomas then also acknowledged the wisdom of the
past.

Subsequently in *Echoes* he wrote, "Everywhere he went, despite his
round collar and his license, he was there to learn rather than teach love."
Even after retirement he continued to serve as supply so that the people
might receive the Sacrament: not that he brought God to them, but that
they could share the bread of love, of life, of truth. "The simplicity of the
Sacrament absolved him from the complexities of the Word."

But he also observed of his retirement: "The problems he had concealed from his congregations had him now all to themselves. A man who
had refrained from quarreling with his parishioners for fear of rhetoric,
over what poetry could he be said to preside from his quarrel with himself" (p. 112). In the second poem of the "Crucifixion" section of *Counterpoint* (1990) he returns to the eucharistic imagery:

> We have over-furnished
> our faith. Our churches
> are as limousines in the procession
> towards heaven. But the verities
> remain: a de-nuclearised
> cross, uncontaminated
> by our coinage; the chalice's
> ichor; and one crumb of bread
> on the tongue for the bird-like
> intelligence to be made tame by.

We can sense here a personal reason, in addition to the pastoral ones
already commented upon, for his conservatism regarding liturgical change.
Struggling with loneliness, with his sense of the silence of God, the famil-

St. Hywyn's, Aberdaron, where Thomas was rector (1967–1978).

iarity of the Eucharist becomes an anchor, a locus point which somehow steadied his erratic orbit. Such a supposition gains force when reading "Bleak Liturgies" in *Mass for Hard Times*.

The title poem of that collection is divided into six parts, each named for a portion of the mass. The sixth section, "Agnus Dei," reads:

> No longer the Lamb
> but the idea of it.
> Can an idea bleed?
> On what altar
> does one sacrifice an idea?
>
> It gave its life
> for the world? No,
> it is we give our life
> for the idea that nourishes
> itself on the dust in our veins.
>
> God is love. Where
> there is no love, no God?
> There is only the gap between
> word and deed we try
> narrowing with an idea.

3.

In using eucharistic imagery, both Herbert and Thomas related the Sacrament to the Crucifixion. For Herbert the Crucifixion vividly demonstrated God's love and the Eucharist, therefore, was an outward and visible reminder of the magnitude and the meaning of that love. Although he wrote in a time when issues of eucharistic theology were matters of great contention, he did not enter the lists of defenders of one position or another. Even so, he did articulate in his poetry the position affirmed by the Thirty-Nine Articles: he believed firmly in the Real Presence and in the efficacy of the Sacrament as a channel of God's grace. This belief provided the energy for his various poems about Holy Communion, as well as his other references to it. In all his references, we find affirmations of God's goodness and redemptive love. At times he also used them to emphasize his own failings and shortcomings as he struggled with his calling, both as a priest and as an individual.

On the other hand, while Thomas's language about the Eucharist is not dissimilar from Herbert's, he used it, not primarily to affirm God's love, but to assert that the Cross is the central *question* of Christianity, in a sense its central — and most difficult — metaphor. Thus, the eucharistic images he invoked are less affirmations of doctrine or of personal penitence, than they are challenges to our hubristic nature. Thomas lived in a century during which the consequences of the scientific revolution were figuratively and literally explosive. And he read and thought much about modern science and technology and contemporary philosophy. However, he remained skeptical of their beneficial character. It would seem difficult for anyone at the turn of the second millennium to believe easily in human progress, that the world is getting better and better. He said (in the Ormond television interview) "In presenting the sacrament, administering the sacrament of bread and wine to the congregation, I am … using a mean, a medium of contact with reality…." For him, the mystery of the Sacrament was a metaphor that raised a series of questions which science, technology, philosophy — all the fruits of human rationality — cannot answer. We can put consecrated bread under an electron microscope and pompously say we have proven there is no real presence, but all we have demonstrated are the limits of our imagination.

> Heaven affords
>   unlimited accommodation
> to the simple-minded.
>   Pardon,

hymn-writers, if levity deputises
                    for an Amen. Too much
has depended on the exigencies
                    of rhyme. You never
improved on 'odd' as the antiphon
                    to a heavenly father.
                                        Tell
me, is truth's victory followed
                    by an armistice?
                                How many
of man's prayers assume
                    an eavesdropping God?
                                        A bishop
            called for an analysis
of the bread and wine. I being
                    no chemist play my recording
of his silence over
                    and over to myself only.
                    —"Revision (II)," *Experimenting with an Amen*

VI

"Faith Makes Me Anything and All"

The consideration of prayer, both corporate and personal, necessarily leads to a consideration of faith, for prayer, by definition, is conversation with the Other and unless there is faith that the Other exists, there can be no conversation, only soliloquy. Chana Bloch has remarked that "One of Herbert's great achievements as a religious poet is to reveal the 'underside' of faith: the difficulty of holding on to what one most deeply believes" (*Spelling the Word*, p. 169). It is a comment that one can as readily, perhaps more readily, apply to Thomas.

"The 'underside' of faith" is doubt: not merely doubt about one's ability to hold "on to what one most deeply believes," but about the very things one believes. However, to recognize doubt as "the 'underside' of faith" is to acknowledge that it is a facet of faith, that rather than being antitheses, they are twinned. The human condition is the condition of the disciple Thomas, "Lord, I believe, help thou my unbelief." The novelist Flannery O'Connor wrote in a letter to a correspondent that doubt is "part of the process by which faith is deepened." She added, "You arrive at enough certainty to be able to make your way, but it is making it in darkness. Don't expect faith to clear things up for you. It is trust, not certainty…" (*The Habit of Being*, pp. 353–354).

Reading the chronicles of faith, whether as ancient as Augustine's *Confessions* or as modern as the journals of Henri Nouwen or Thomas Merton, we encounter examples of O'Connor's description of doubt's integral relation with its sister, faith. Both Herbert and Thomas describe vividly that same experience — vividly enough that one knows they have lived it themselves.

1.

The poem which immediately precedes the eloquent "Prayer (I)" ("Prayer the Churches banquet...") in *The Temple* is "Faith," suggesting that it is faith which leads to prayer. It begins:

> Lord, how couldst thou so much appease
> Thy wrath for sinne as, when mans sight was dimme
> And could see little, to regard his ease,
> And bring by Faith all things to him?

It is a question that the poem does not answer and, in declining to answer it, Herbert moved toward the nature of faith. That movement brought him finally to say in the closing stanza:

> What though my bodie runne to dust?
> Faith cleaves unto it, counting ev'ry grain
> With an exact and most particular trust,
> Reserving all for flesh again.

On the way to this resolution, the fifth and sixth stanzas provide a moving description of the sense and quality of faith:

> Faith makes me any thing, or all
> That I beleeve is in the sacred storie:
> And where sinne placeth me in Adams fall,
> Faith sets me higher in his glorie.

> If I go lower in the book,
> What can be lower than the common manger?
> Faith puts me there with him, who sweetly took
> Our flesh and frailtie, death and danger.

Thus, Herbert acknowledged both what faith does and the reality of our lives, that there is an ebb and flow, times of fullness and times when we "go lower in the book."

The structure of the whole manuscript elucidates this understanding. "Faith" appears early in the sequence of poems (it is the 19th of 160) and immediately follows "Affliction (I)" and "Repentance." Those poems are part of the broader pattern of faith that "rises and falls like the tides of an invisible ocean," to borrow again from O'Connor. And as we continue to read through *The Temple*, the pattern becomes clearer. Each step forward, each affirmation of faith, seems to be followed by recession, by confusion, by doubt. Herbert limned the pattern in the opening stanza of "The Temper (I)":

> How should I praise thee, Lord! how should my rymes
>   Gladly engrave thy love in steel,
>   If what my soul doth feel sometimes,
>   My soul might ever feel!

The "exact and particular trust" of faith is a sometimes thing. In moments of grief and affliction, we may yet feel assurance that, in spite of all, God's grace will "drop from above." Yet, at other moments, the afflictions seem too much, the clanking of the chains of our own mortality too raucous, the inconstancies of our thoughts too distracting, to allow us to rest in faith. In such moments we suffer, as Herbert did, the silence of God. In the five poems entitled "Affliction," all occurring within the first half of *The Temple*, or the later "Miserie," "Dulnesse," and "Longing," Herbert described the onset of these descents to the underside of faith. Always, however, his sense of the silence of God manifested doubt, a fraying of trust, not about the existence of God, but about the purpose and meaning of his own life. He doubted that he could serve God, or rather that God could use him: he doubted then the qualities of God — and His intentions.

The pattern ultimately, however, is not circular, but spiral. The movement, for all the falling back, the ebbing, is forward, nearer. Man is always turning, turning again. Conversion is a continuous process:

> Lord, mend or rather make us: one creation
>   Will not suffice our turn:
> Except thou make us dayly, we shall spurn
>   Our own salvation.
>   — "Giddinesse"

The pilgrimage of faith is a long and weary way, marked by stumblings, wanderings from the path, seeming relapses. Yet there is also incremental growth in understanding, in acceptance of both joys and sorrows as redemptive, in trust.

This is the pattern that ultimately gives *The Temple* its unity, the pattern of the spiritual life as we actually experience it. Diogenes Allen argued that the poem "Coloss. 3.3. Our life is hid with Christ in God" is central to Herbert's view of the workings of divine providence and so to his whole vision for his manuscript (my notes from seminar on Herbert, St. Deiniol's Research Library, August, 2000):

> *My* words & thoughts do both expresse this notion,
> That *Life* hath with the sun a double motion.
> The first *Is* straight, and our diurnall friend,
> The other *Hid* and doth obliquely bend.
> One life is wrapt *In* flesh, and tends to earth:
> The other winds toward *Him*, whose happie birth
> Taught me to live here so, *That* still one eye
> Should aim and shoot at that which *Is* on high:
> Quitting with daily labour all *My* pleasure,
> To gain at harvest an eternall *Treasure*.

By words and structure the poem reveals the relationship between our daily lives and our spiritual lives. Everything in the course of our lives, read as the horizontal lines of the poem, contributes to the progression of our spiritual lives. We may not know, we often do not know, which actions (words) most contribute to God's purpose for us, but even those which do, require the other words and spaces to have their effect. We tread the horizontal and can have no clear sense of the whole until the end — if then. The spiritual life is not entirely hidden, but some of the ways God works are. Not that they are separate from our daily lives, only that we do not recognize them. Thus the hard moments — of sorrow, of doubt, of suffering God's silence, even absence — are integral to a life of faith. Thus, too, the spiritual life is not purely interior, but is expressed in and through what we do daily in our relations with others, faith active in love.

The Temple is not a manual instructing us how to live the spiritual life. Rather, it is a description of the reality of that life, of the twistings and turnings, the fullness and the emptiness, the high meadows and the dark valleys of faith.

2.

In a television interview in the 1970s, R. S. Thomas described his work by saying, "Primarily, I'm trying to find out what it means to use the word 'God' in the late twentieth century with all the discoveries and changes which have come about in the human intellect." That is an observation seemingly bathed in skepticism and indicates that for him the "'underside' of faith" was both darker and broader than for Herbert. It involved not only "the difficulty of holding on to what one most deeply believes," but the possibility of belief itself. It is the silence of God, even the absence of God, which seemed the most redoubtable quality of the divine. And the most striking—to some readers and critics—the most daunting quality of Thomas's poetry was the doggedness with which he pursued his task.

While Thomas's earliest collections (*The Stones of the Field*, 1946, and *An Acre of Land*, 1952) are predominantly about the life of rural Wales, gritty pastorals, his last (*Mass for Hard Times*, 1992, and *No Truce with the Furies*, 1995) are preoccupied with the issues of faith and doubt, life and death, that go by the term "religious." Yet the seeds were there in the beginning for that stubborn pursuit of truths which pass man's understanding. Consider, for example, the brief elegy about the church at Manafon ("Country Church"):

> The church stands, built from the river stone,
> Brittle with light, as though a breath could shatter
> Its slender frame, or spill the limpid water,
> Quiet as sunlight, cupped within the bone.
>
> It stands yet. But though soft flowers break
> In delicate waves round limbs the river fashioned
> With so smooth care, no friendly God has cautioned
> The brimming tides of fescue for its sake.

Or the equally moving description of an abandoned chapel in "Maes-yr-Onnen," that concludes:

> You cannot hear as I, incredulous, heard
> Up in the rafters, where the bell should ring,
> The wild, sweet singing of Rhiannon's birds.

Both poems combine spare evocation of a place where faith once blossomed with a mystical sense of nature, proleptic of the recurring question of absence/presence.

Those seeds sent forth roots deep in the soil of Wales and the creative instincts of the poet to produce a rich and varied crop over almost five decades. Thomas published some collections unrelated to his explorations of "what it means to use the word 'God'" (for example, *What Is a Welshman?*, 1974), and individual poems within his collections may appear discursions from that pursuit, but he has ceaselessly returned to the quest.

St. Michael and All Angels's, Manafon, where Thomas was rector (1942–1953).

As already noted, the very titles of many of his collections suggest, not only the tentative quality of individual poems, but also the probing, questioning, nature of his enterprise. The various poems about prayer amply illustrate Thomas's sense of the silence of God, and often in shadowy moments the poet wonders whether silence is indeed absence.

In "The Absence" (*Frequencies*) we find perhaps the most moving depiction of this theme:

> It is this great absence
> that is like a presence, that compels
> me to address it without hope
> of a reply. It is a room I enter
>
> from which someone has just
> gone, the vestibule for the arrival
> of one who has not yet come.
> I modernise the anachronism
>
> of my language, but he is no more here
> than before. Genes and molecules
> have no more power to call
> him up than the incense of the Hebrews

at their altars. My equations fail
as my words do. What resource have I
other than the emptiness without him of my whole
being, a vacuum he may not abhor?

This collection, appearing as it did just as Thomas retired from his last
cure in Aberdaron, provides a stunning gloss on the laconic observation
he later published in *The Echoes Return Slow*:

> The problems he had concealed from his congregations had him
> now all to themselves. A man who had refrained from quarrelling
> with his parishioners for fear of rhetoric, over what poetry could
> he be said to preside from his quarrel with himself [p. 112]?

As he scanned the dial, he experienced "the eternal / silence that is the
repose of God" ("The Gap"). That is how he opened the collection. He concluded it thusly:

Was the pilgrimage
I made to come to my own
self, to learn that in times
like these and for one like me
God will never be plain and
out there, but dark rather and
inexplicable, as though he were in here?

Questions, always questions. He seems relentless in his asking. He is
as despairing as Herbert often is. But there is this about him, a willing-
ness to question everything — including his own doubt. So he struggles on,
making *No Truce with the Furies*.

Young I visited
this pool; asked my question,
passed on. In the middle years
visited it again. The question
had sunk down, hardly
a ripple. To be no longer
young, yet not to be old
is a calm without
equal. The water ticks on,
but time stands, fingerless.

Today, thirty years
later, on the margin
of eternity, dissolution,
nothing but the self
looking up at the self
looking down, with each
refusing to become
an object, so with the Dane's
help, from bottomless fathoms
I dredge up the truth.
                        —"Fathoms"

The reference to Søren Kierkegaard indicates one of the important resources for Thomas in his ponderings of life's meaning. There are others, numerous others: the Bible, Wallace Stevens, and William Butler Yeats are but a few. He sought from them, not answers, but assistance in forming the questions. In a letter to Alfred Corn, Flannery O'Connor wrote, "Learn what you can, but cultivate Christian skepticism. It will keep you free — not free to do anything you please, but free to be formed by something larger than your own intellect or the intellects of those around you" (*The Habit of Being*, p. 478).

                    And the mind,
        then, weary of the pilgrimages
        to its horizons— is there no spring of thought
        adjacent to it, where it can be
        dipped, so that emerging but
        once in ten thousand times,
        freed of its crutches, is sufficient
        testimony to the presence in it
        of a power other than its own?
                —"Cures," *Experimenting with an Amen*

Amidst all the persistent questioning, the catalogues of interrogatories, the explorations of this "'underside' of faith," we encounter still points in Thomas's poetry, moments of shining calm that define the quality of faith. Like the "sweet singing of Rhiannon's birds," we hear it in "Echoes," "The Presence," "The Bright Field," "Suddenly," in the closing lines from *Counterpoint*, or these from *The Echoes Return Slow*:

> At times
> in the silence between
> prayers, after the Amens
> fade, at the world's
> centre, it is as though
> love stands, renouncing itself.

The meaning is in the waiting, in doubt and in faith.

3.

   Both Herbert and Thomas found their poetic voice in arguments with themselves and with God. For Herbert the arguments were intensely personal, manifestations of his struggle to submit himself to overcome his own prideful sense of unworthiness, to discern and submit himself to God's will. He identified as his life's motto (posie) a passage from Genesis 32:10:

> Let wits contest,
> And with their words and posies windows fill:
>   *Lesse then the least*
> *Of all thy mercies*, is my posie still.

> This on my ring,
> This by my picture, in my book I write:
>   Whether I sing,
> Or say, or dictate, this is my delight.

> Invention rest,
> Comparisons go play, wit use thy will:
>   *Lesse then the least*
> *Of all Gods mercies*, is my posie still.
>   —"The Posie"

His poetic voice is akin to Thomas the Doubter. His poems have predominately the quality of prayer, of petition, of praise and of thanksgiving. If God wills that they speak to others, help others through their own dark valleys, so be it.

   While R. S. Thomas certainly expressed his own mind and heart, the argument was less interior, more distinctly spoken of the human condition and more directly spoken to the world. His is less the voice of prayer than the voice of Job. In one of his earliest published poems, reprinted in his first collection, *The Stones of the Field*, but not in any of the subsequent gatherings of his work, he wrote:

> Who is skilled to read
> The strange epitaph of the salt weed
> Scrawled on our shores? Who can make plain
> The thin, dark characters of rain,
> Or the hushed speech of wind and star
> In the deep-throated fir?
>
> Was not this the voice that lulled
> Job's seething mind to a still calm,
> Yet tossed his heart to the racked world?
> —"The Question"

If for poetic reasons Thomas subsequently found this poem wanting, it nonetheless set the tone for his long and stubborn quest.

Thomas described both Herbert and himself, at least figuratively, when he said, "Over every poet's door is nailed Keats's saying about negative capability. Poetry is born of the tension set up by the poet's ability to be 'in uncertainties, mysteries, doubts, without any irritable reaching after fact and reason'" (*The Penguin Book of Religious Verse*, p. 11).

VII

"One Cunning Bosome-sinne"

Herbert and Thomas shared a sense, not only of the imperfection of human beings, but of their imperfectibility. It is, as it were, in the nature of the beast. Put more bluntly in language that is less fashionable today, both had a sense of the sinfulness of man and for both the nature and actuality of sin informed their poetry. Of course, both were also priests, so what can you expect? One recalls the anecdote about Calvin Coolidge that goes something like this: after church one Sunday reporters asked him what the minister had preached about. Coolidge responded, "Sin." "Well, what did he say about it?" "He was against it." Herbert and Thomas operate within the Christian theological framework and are surely against sin, but their poetic eloquence deserves more reflection than Coolidge apparently gave the preacher — or, too often, we give to theological understandings of the nature of man. In a world in which we seem wont to ascribe the evils that men do to "inadequate socialization" or rationalize our own shortcomings, we might do well to ponder anew what ancient wisdoms tell us on the subject.

1.

Whether or not one views the narrative "I" of *The Temple* as the poet himself in his various several selves, the poetry is an account of spiritual conflicts. In particular those conflicts arise from a sense of human inadequacies, that is, quite simply, sinfulness, for sin is an absence, a deficiency, not an added quality. That deficiency produces the erratic quality of the Christian's spiritual life, the seemingly constant stumblings and fallings and risings again. One of the earliest poems (the 6th of 159) in "The Church," the main body of *The Temple*, is "The Sinner."

Lord, how I am all ague, when I seek
　　What I have treasur'd in my memorie!
　　Since, if my soul make even with the week,
Each seventh note by right is due to thee.
I find there quarries of pil'd vanities,
　　But shreds of holinesse, that dare not venture
　　To shew their face, since crosse to thy decrees:
There the circumference earth is, heav'n the centre.
In so much dregs the quintessence is small:
　　The spirit and good extract of my heart
　　Comes to about the many hundred part.
Yet Lord restore thine image, heare my call:
　　And though my hard heart scarce to thee can grone,
　　Remember that thou once didst write in stone.

Knowing what we do of the character of Herbert, we may find the
intensity of his contrition overwrought — I suspect it may be one of the
reasons why Thomas said he no longer could read him — but we need to
consider it in the context of the rhetoric of the time. And we need also to
remember that he had a powerful sense, not simply of his own sins, but
of the sinful nature of all men, that while he was writing from his experience he was speaking to the experience of all those who strive to live the
spiritual life. And, of course, in the reading of the poem, the reader
becomes the narrator. It was not that Herbert regarded himself as pecu-
liarly or abnormally sinful, rather he was simply all too human as evident
in the closing stanzas of "Miserie":

　　Indeed at first Man was a treasure,
A box of jewels, shop of rarities,
　　A ring, whose posie was, *My pleasure:*
He was a garden in a Paradise:
　　　　Glorie and grace
　　　　Did crown his heart and face.

　　But sinne hath fool'd him. Now he is
A lump of flesh, without a foot or wing
　　To raise him to a glimpse of blisse:
A sick toss'd vessel, dashing on each thing;
　　　　Nay his own shelf:
　　　　My God, I mean my self.

This latter poem follows immediately on "Affliction (V)," "Mortification," and "Decay," forming one of the recurrent recessions into despair which will then turn to a buoyant affirmation of God's goodness and grace. They seem together a declaration of man's depravity in accord with Calvinism. Yet there is also a persistent sense (as described in the poem "Man" which precedes this sequence) that, though wanting, we are yet noble creations of God. It is the tension between what we are and what we could be that gives his poems a universal quality. To reiterate C. S. Lewis's observation, he described "the very quality of life as we actually live it moment by moment." He did so, however, in the language of the Christian faith, and more particularly in the language of the seventeenth-century English church with its overlays of reformed theology. Therefore, the idea of the sinfulness of man was a given.

> Lord, with what care hast thou begirt us round!
>   Parents first season us: then schoolmasters
>   Deliver us to laws; they send us bound
> To rules of reason, holy messengers,
> Pulpits and Sundayes, sorrow dogging sinne,
>   Afflictions sorted, anguish of all sizes,
>   Fine nets and strategems to catch us in,
> Bibles laid open, millions of surprises,
> Blessings beforehand, tyes of gratefulnesse,
>   The sound of glorie ringing in our eares;
>   Without, our shame; within, our consciences;
> Angels and grace, eternall hopes and fears.
>   Yet all these fences and their whole aray
>   One cunning bosome-sinne blows quite away.
>   —"Sinne (I)"

The call to a devout and holy life in an avowedly religious community is clear and repetitive. The appeal of such a life, both positive and negative, may seem protection enough against temptation, but "one cunning bosome-sinne" can undo it all. Perfection, after all, must be perfect, and within the heart of every human lies the potential for, indeed a preference for, imperfection.

Earlier, in writing about the evolution of Herbert's calling, I noted that in writing "Sinne (I)" he may have been remembering the time earlier in his life when he had sought help from Sir Francis Nethersol in obtaining the position of University Orator. Nethersol expressed the fear that "this place being civil ... [it might] draw me too much from Divinity …," but Herbert, with youthful confidence, replied "that this dignity, hath no such earthiness in it, but it may very well be joined with Heaven; or if it had to others, yet to me it should not" (*Works*, p. 370). Later, Herbert would charge himself with false humility. In the earlier case the "cunning bosome-sinne" of pride wore no mask.

We know that Herbert labored over the sequencing of his poems and that there is a rhythm within the whole body of "The Church." For example, "The Sinner" immediately follows "The Agonie" and directly precedes his "Good Friday" poems. The former, in effect, declares that if you want to know what sin is look to the agony of the crucified and if you want to know what love is look to the crucified. "Good Friday" absorbs the general affirmation of the first and the particulars of "The Sinner" to affirm, without using the term, the doctrine of the Atonement. And Herbert moved from there to his Easter poems. Similarly, "Sinne (I)" immediately follows a poem ("Nature") in which he asserted the human preference for imperfection: "Full of rebellion, I would die, / Or fight, or travell, or denie / That thou hast ought to do with me." Then he prays that God might "tame my heart, … smooth my rugged heart, … Or make a new one." And it immediately precedes a poem ("Affliction [I]") in which he described the ebb and flow of his spiritual health from a time when "There was no month but May," to one in which "Sorrow was all my soul." In turn, that poem is followed by "Repentance" and the joyous "Faith."

These clusters have a similar dynamic. If this were a musical composition one might think of them as theme and variation, and as in music the variation adds to the theme. C. S. Lewis made this observation about grief:

> [It] … is like a long valley, a winding valley where any bend may reveal a totally new landscape…. Not every bend does. Sometimes … you are presented with exactly the same sort of country you thought you had left behind miles ago. That is when you wonder whether the valley isn't a circular trench. But it isn't. There are partial recurrences, but the sequence doesn't repeat [*A Grief Observed*, p. 47].

One could say the same of the "picture of the many spiritual conflicts" which Herbert created with his poetry. The structure of the composition plays out, not a repetitive melody, but moves forward toward a resolution. As a whole it provides us the sound and sense of the Christian pilgrimage.

In a second poem also entitled "Sinne," Herbert wrote:

> O That I could a sinne once see!
> We paint the devil foul, yet he
> Hath some good in him all agree.

Sinne is flat opposite to th'Almightie, seeing
It wants the good of *vertue*, and of *being*.

But God more care of us hath had:
If apparitions make us sad,
By sight of sinne we should grow mad.
Yet as in sleep we see foul death, and live:
So devils are our sinnes in perspective.

I will admit to some difficulty with this poem, both poetically and theologically. Apparently, Thomas did as well for, though in his selection of Herbert's verse he included "The Sinner," "Sinne (I)" and "Sinnes Round," he omitted this one. ("The Sinner" is also one of four Herbert poems Thomas includes in *The Penguin Book of Religious Verse*. It is obviously a poem he "found satisfactory in itself.") And perhaps the theological problems derive from the poetic ones. Poetically it is less memorable than "Sinne (I)" and it is less clear. F. E. Hutchinson, editor of the now standard edition of Herbert, provided an extended footnote citing Augustine and Aquinas as providing the clue to the poem. As apt as his observation is, it does not alleviate the fact that the poem does not work. It suggests that if we could actually see our sins "in the flesh" as it were, we would be so revulsed that we would go mad, but God is gentler than that. Instead of seeing sin itself incarnate we see devils, "Our sinnes in perspective," a bad enough sight, but one that allows us to understand the nature of sin. Perhaps it is my modern — though not too modern — sensibility that leads me to say that the "devils" we see are devilish people and, perhaps more often, the consequences of sinful behavior, including our own.

More striking than the poem itself is its placement: it follows close upon "Affliction (II)" and is bracketed by "Mattens" and "Even-song." "Affliction (II)" rather than recounting Herbert's own spiritual life, in effect, declares that all his pains, all his sorrows — indeed the pains and sorrows of all humans — are paltry compared to those of Christ on the cross, and are subsumed by His grief. The poems which stand each side of "Sinne (II)," like the services of matins and evensong, are anthems to the Divine Love. Hutchinson remarked that the reason for the placement of this poem between the other two is unclear. That very placement, however, gives the most sense to the poem, for it there appears as a specific illustration of the gentleness of God's love in dealing with us.

The spiral dynamic of Herbert's *Temple*, the sense of moving upward in a circular pattern, is turned on its head in the poem "Sinnes Round."

Sorrie I am, my God, sorrie I am,
That my offences course it in a ring.
My thoughts are working like a busie flame,
Untill their cockatrice they hatch and bring:
And when they once have perfected their draughts,
My words take fire from my inflamed thoughts.

My words take fire from my inflamed thoughts,
Which spit it forth like the Sicilian Hill,
They vent the wares, and passe them with their faults,
And by their breathing ventilate the ill.
But words suffice not, where there are lewd intentions:
My hands do joyn to finish the inventions.

My hands do joyn to finish the inventions:
And so my sinnes ascend three stories high,
As Babel grew, before there were dissensions.
Till ill deeds loyter not: for they supplie
New thoughts of sinning: wherefore, to my shame,
Sorrie I am, my God, sorrie I am.

This round dance/song does not move in a circle, but in a downward spiral. As the very weight of sins piles up, the theme moves from an expression of contrition, the opening "Sorrie I am, my God, sorrie I am," to a confession of baseness, the closing "Sorrie I am, my God, sorrie I am." In his *"This Book of Starres,"* James Boyd White suggested the downward spiral is countered by the narrator's growing awareness of his condition. What makes this contrapuntal quality effective is less the work of the individual poem than it is of the whole architecture (or compositional structure) of Herbert's manuscript.

One could go on, for the sense of sinfulness, both his own and mankind's, is ubiquitous in Herbert, but it is almost invariably linked with the consciousness of God's love, a love most manifest in the Cross.

2.

R. S. Thomas published about nine hundred poems over his lifetime, roughly half of which were republished in his *Collected Poems, 1945–1990* (1993). Nowhere among these many poems do we find one entitled "Sin" or "The Sinner," though there are several entitled "Pardon" and one "Absolution." Even the word "sin" does not often appear in his poems, but the reality is there, both the strong sense of the sinfulness of man and the naming of specific sins, most particularly acts of pride and avarice. As he states in his introduction to the Penguin anthology, "Without the darkness, in the world we know, the light would go unprized; without evil, goodness would have no meaning" (p. 11).

In his long early poem, "The Minister," Thomas powerfully illustrates the harshness and cruelty of life in the hardscrabble world of the hills:

> 'Beloved, let us love one another,' the words are blown
> To pieces by the unchristened wind
> In the chapel rafters, and love's text
> Is riddled by the inhuman cry
> Of buzzards circling above the moor.

"Take my advice," says the chapel deacon Job Davies ("a master / hand at choosing a nag or a pastor,") "Pick someone young, and I'll soon show him / How things is managed in the hills here."

The story told is of a serious, earnest young man, newly graduated from college, moved by the freshness of his vocation, but ignorant "Of the bare moor … [and] the names / Of the birds and flowers by which one gets / A little closer to nature's heart." He preaches vigorously of Sin and imagines he has "made a neat job / On pruning the branches on the tree / Of good and evil." But when he tried to speak to Davies about a sin, the deacon's adultery, Davies replies, "Take a word from me and keep your nose / In the Black Book, so it won't be tempted / To go sniffing where it's not wanted…." And "The rhythm of the seasons: wind and rain / Dryness and heat, and then the wind again…," like the sullen looks he met, the waning of enthusiasm, the utter loneliness, wore him down. "I knew and pretended I didn't. / And they knew that I knew and pretended I didn't. / They listened to me preaching the unique gospel / Of love; but our eyes never met." So he sickens and dies: the victim of both the narrowness of his own soul and the "sly infirmities" of his people.

While it would be comfortable, sitting in an academic study or a glitzy coffee bar, to think of Thomas as a "rural poet" and dismiss "The Minister" as a bucolic tale having little to do with the reality of life in a modern, technological society, such a judgement misses the universal quality at its core, the sharply etched observations about human nature that give the poem its true eloquence. It also fails to take proper account of the mind of the poet, for he understood modern science and technology — and he also understood that scientists and engineers and technocrats and politicians and theologians are first of all human beings before they are any of those things.

Time and again, in his poems, he remarks upon our failures, our missing the mark, because we are what we are, all too human. In the "Kyrie" from the title poem of *Mass for Hard Times,* he writes:

> Because we cannot be clever and honest
> and are inventors of things more intricate
> than the snowflake — Lord have mercy.
>
> Because we are full of pride
> in our humility, and because we believe
> in our disbelief — Lord have mercy.
>
> Because we will protect ourselves
> from ourselves to the point
> of destroying ourselves — Lord have mercy.
>
> And because on the slope to perfection,
> when we should be half-way up,
> we are half-way down — Lord have mercy.

There is, as well, more here than an amorphous expression of the "tragic sense of life." It is not cosmic fatality, but the real imperfections of people, which bring the sorrow and the pain, and not only to the Reverend Elias Morgan, B. A. Thomas began the poem "Covenant" from *Between Here and Now* (1981) thusly:

> I feel sometimes
>   we are his penance
> for having made us. He
> suffers in us and we partake
>   of his suffering. What
> to do, when it has been done
>   already?...

The poem bristles with the sense of man's affinity for sin, and, like so many of Thomas's poems, has at least the shadow of the shadow of the Cross cast across its lines. Implicit is the Atonement.

It is not an easy doctrine, but one that Thomas came at time and again, sometimes directly, sometimes obliquely, never quite embracing joyously, but never able to turn away from it. He addressed it in one of the early poems of the collection *Laboratories of the Spirit*:

It was all arranged:
the virgin with child, the birth
in Bethlehem, the arid journey uphill
to Jerusalem. The prophets foretold
it, the scriptures conditioned him
to accept it. Judas went to his work
with his sour kiss; what else
could he do?
          A wise old age,
the honours awarded for lasting,
are not for a saviour. He had
to be killed; salvation acquired
by an increased guilt. The tree,
with its roots in the mind's dark,
was divinely planted, the original fork
in existence. There is no meaning in life
unless men can be found to reject
love. God needs his martyrdom.
The mild eyes stare from the Cross
in perverse triumph. What does he care
that the people's offerings are so small?
                   —"Amen"

The first eight lines reduce the story to its bare essentials with an almost "Can you believe this?" tone, which, throughout, approaches doubt, yet always under the arch of the title "Amen," i.e. "So be it." Even at the edge of irony, the tone is not dismissive, for Thomas was never content with the answers of faithless rationality, any more than with those of irrational faith. The Cross demands more than that because "There is no meaning in life / unless men can be found to reject / love"—and there is no lack of such men.

In writing of Herbert I have commented at length on the groupings and ordering of his poems, suggesting a spiral dynamic, returning to themes/questions/concerns, yet never quite repeating. One detects something of the same quality in Thomas. The stanza quoted above from "Covenant" ends "... Circularity / is a mental condition, the / animals know nothing of." But elsewhere, in the opening poem of the collection from which "Amen" comes, he observed "... Circular as our way / is, it leads not back to the snake-haunted / garden, but onward to the tall city / of glass that is the laboratory of the spirit." In the laboratory one constantly changes the variables, testing hypotheses, eliminating possibilities, and repeating and repeating to verify conclusions. Thus, Thomas proceeded, circling, assaying, trying to move closer to understanding, to knowing. And in the end, only

> I think that maybe
> I will be a little surer
> of being a little nearer.
> That's all. Eternity
> is in the understanding
> that that little is more than enough.
> — *Counterpoint* (1990)

3.

In *The Temple* Herbert makes no specific reference to contemporary political events, yet in the context of his sense of human sinfulness we should consider a conviction which he shared with Thomas to which I briefly referred in the introduction, namely pacifism. Discussing Herbert's call to the priesthood, Joseph Summers detailed Herbert's adherence to the pacific policy that James I pursued over the hawkish policy Prince Charles (and many others) pressed in the wake of the failure of negotiations for a marriage alliance with Spain. He made his adherence clear in the oration he gave welcoming Charles back. (*George Herbert. His Religion and His Art*, pp. 40–42.) At roughly the same time (1623) Herbert wrote a long poem in Latin, "Triumphus Mortis" ("The Triumph of Death") tracing the origin of death to anger fed by selfish pride (and wine). Quite simply war resulted from man's sin. (The following translations are from Mark McCloskey and Paul R. Murphy, *The Latin Poetry of George Herbert*.)

> Killing, unrefined, rude, was not enough: a talent
> For death was sought, and the learned killer
> Came into vogue. And so recruits, young men
> Used to scanty rations, makeshift Goddess of War
> And the sports of authentic war, battle lines
> Deployed, winters braved in skins—all these
> That men might gouge unblamed through ribs
> And get their fame as the artisans
> And graduates of death....

He recounted the "progress" of war in its increasing savagery:

Still the world had not the engine
Most worthy of the sins of men.
No age will swear at it enough: metal glowing
In the red kiln liquefies, and bubbling down
In the worn grooves, the iron-water pours:
The tube emerges, and the monster emerges
With a single eye, in the likeness
Of Homer's Cyclops, rejoices in the hole bored
In the middle. Then wheels and axles take the burden up
Like a curule chair, and from it
Death sitting, triumphs over man.

One wonders what scorching words he would have found for our even more brutal and devastating engines of war.

If anything, the oration he delivered on Charles's return from Spain without a bride and to vociferous cries for war presents an even sharper and lurid picture. Amid all the formulaic celebration of Charles's safe restoration to England, Herbert declared:

> Know you not, I pray, the miseries of war?... Slaughterings of every kind, mangled bodies, the mutilated image of God, a little span of life long enough for weeping, the burning of cities, crashings, plunderings, violated virgins, women with child twice killed, little infants shedding more milk than blood; images, nay shadows of men, with hunger, cold, filth, vext, crushed, disabled. How cruel is glory which is reared upon the necks of men; when it is doubtful whether he who achieves it, or he who suffers, is the more miserable [Marchette Chute, *Two Gentle Men*, p. 84].

Given the vigor of Herbert's conviction, the absence of any specific evidence of it in *The Temple* is striking. The only reference to things military occurs in "The Church-porch" and has a peculiar blandness to it:

Art thou a Magistrate? then be severe:
If studious, copie fair, what time hath blurr'd;
Redeem truth from his jawes: if souldier,
Chase brave employments with a naked sword
Throughout the world. Fool not: for all may have,
If they dare try, a glorious life, or grave.
                                   — ll. 85–90

There is, however, no mitigation of his sense of man's sinfulness. If he did not articulate his pacifism in *The Temple*, it is because his purpose did not require it. He was concerned not with matters of state, but with the individual soul's experience in everyday life and under the shadow of God's redeeming love.

In "Neb" Thomas states "R. S. had been a pacifist on principle ever since finding himself at Chirk before the Second World War." He does not explain the details of his decision except to cite the influence of Hewlett Johnson, Dean of Canterbury Cathedral, and observing it was a position "fitting for a priest." He also recalled writing to friends at the time of the Munich crisis saying "God would not allow something as terrible as war." Though events quickly proved the naivete of that remark he remained a pacifist throughout the war. In the aftermath of it he became active in the Campaign for Nuclear Disarmament. To him the "bomb was a *reductio ad absurdem*," his argument made prosaically echoing Herbert's "Triumphus Mortis."

Yet he also recognized a tension between his pacifism and his desire "for something approaching Welsh freedom or self-rule." It was a tension that persisted. Though he never advocated force, the Welsh equivalent of the IRA, he was criticized for not condemning the extremist campaign of burning English summer cottages—or not condemning it vigorously enough. His seeming reluctance to do so derived not simply from his Welsh nationalism, but also from his understanding of the nature of the world in which he lived. He wrote:

> Farmers are used to the dirty side of life. Killing is part of their way of life. Catching and killing rabbits was a weekly necessity in Manafon, on account of their great numbers at the time. On a threshing day, before reaching the bottom of the rick, the men and the boys and the dogs would prepare for an attack on the hundreds of rats hiding there. The young rector would himself see the birds of prey hunting, and the weasel and the stoat going about their bloody work. And how beautiful those birds are, and how agile the small animals that hunt. Anyone who has seen a peregrine falcon falling like lightning on its prey is sure to experience a certain thrill that makes him feel quite humble. These are the masters of the world of nature. One of the unfailing rules of that world is that life has to die in the cause of life. If there is any other way on this earth, God has not seen fit to follow it. This is a doctrine that plays straight into the hands of the strong. As far as this world is concerned, Isaiah's vision of the wolf dwelling with the lamb, and the leopard lying down with the kid is a myth [*Autobiographies*, pp. 95–96].

If he was a poet of nature, a "nature mystic" even, he was not a romantic. Yet to recognize the cruel realities of the natural world was not to condone them, nor to see the "rules of life" for the beasts as commandments for humankind. If there is much that it is beautiful in nature, merely the contemplation of those beauties is not salvific. In *The Echoes Return Slow* he says:

> From meditation on a flower
> you think more flowers will be born
> of your mind? Eichmann meditated
> on music and played on his
>
> victims' limbs the symphony
> of perdition. I have watched
> the tendrils of flowers with less strength
> than a child's fingers opening
>
> the hard rock. You know what flowers
> do best on. I think how the bodies
> of the centuries have been rendered down
> that this one should emerge, innocent of
>   compassion.

If there is much to learn from nature, man was not made in the image of the wolf or the leopard, or the lamb or the kid, or even the flower. The violence of nature should be a negative example, not one to imitate.

Nor was Thomas willing to accept the easy justification of war as a "necessary evil." Like his dogged pursuit of the silent God, he held to his pacifism because violence, if sometimes understandable, was nonetheless wrong, a manifestation of man's sinfulness.

> Wanting peace we were misled
> by a dead nation's counsel
> to prepare for war. Thinking love
> would survive an instruction
> in violence, we took ourselves back
> to a dark school, terrified
> ourselves with our own propaganda.
>
> As Germans their nostrils
> with bad smells, we inoculated
> ourselves with the poison factories
> of our meadows. Our scientists
> had white coats, vestments
> these of their clandestine ritual.

> Somewhere from under an old
> dustbin lid you will have emerged
> for the re-assembling of the species.
> We have left you nothing
> but the consequences of our refusal
> to sit down by the still pool
> in the mind, waiting for the unknown
> visitant's quickening of its surface.
> —"Bequest," *Destinations*

Here is a dark vision of the future, one that sees the consequences of man's using the greatest of his gifts to pursue bestial ends— power, dominance, control — as destructive. Here too a cry in the wilderness of man's making to another, not a cry for help, but a confession of our failure.

Throughout Thomas's poetry we find references to the ravages of war, yet he did not write what we might call pacifist poetry. To call it that is as limiting and inadequate as to label him a rural poet or a Welsh nationalist, or even a religious poet, when what we mean by that reflects not what he wrote, but the limits of our own imaginations. His references to war decry its results, but he viewed war as only one manifestation, though an egregious one, of our failures— just as his plaints about technology are not the words of a modern Luddite, but a reminder that we have misused the fruit of our labors.

In *H'm* he offers this terse summary of twentieth-century history:

> Mostly it was wars
> With their justification
> Of the surrender of values
> For which they fought. Between
> Them they laid their plans
> For the next, exempted
> From compact by the machine's
> Exigencies. Silence
> Was out of date; wisdom consisted
> In a revision of the strict code
> Of the spirit. To keep moving
> Was best, to bring the arrival
> Nearer departure; to synchronise
> The applause, as the public images
> Stepped on and off the stationary
> Aircraft. The labour of the years

Was over; the children were heirs
To an instant existence. They fed the machine
Their questions, knowing the answers
Already, unable to apply them.

                              —"Digest"

4.

Both Herbert and Thomas accepted the reality of sin, in the general sense of man's propensity to do evil and in the specific sense of their own personal shortcomings. Not surprisingly Herbert was more preoccupied with the latter. While he often spoke universally, he made no specific references to events in the broader world around him that might have illustrated human sinfulness, and precious few which even allusively might be considered as responses to political or social injustices. Rather he described the spiritual struggle of an individual soul and that story has universal meaning and value precisely because of its particularity.

In contrast, while also recounting his own struggles of the spirit, quarrels even, Thomas was much more attentive to the exterior world. Of course, he was more consciously speaking to the world than was Herbert, who, in a sense, was a diarist. Having actively published his poems for almost six decades, Thomas accepted the public, one might say bardic, responsibility of the poet. Some critics have suggested he is too much preoccupied with evil and suffering in the world, an odd and ultimately unfair complaint about someone writing in the last half of the twentieth century. One suspects that the real problem for such critics is that Thomas, no less than Herbert, not only accepted the imperfectibility of man, but also possessed an unquenchable thirst for God.

In the face of the disorder and distemper of the world, plagued as it is with man's sinfulness, Thomas, like Herbert, turned back to the particular, to scratching at the hard questions of daily living, to hymning the small virtues of life that make true heroes.

And courage shall give way
to despair and despair
to suffering, and suffering
shall end in death. But you
who are not free to choose
what you suffer can choose
your response....

                    —"The Unvanquished," *Destinations*

VIII

"Love Bade Me Welcome": "Love Fiercer Than We Can Understand"

While the weight of sin is equally evident in the poetry of Herbert and Thomas, there is a great disparity between the two poets in terms of the attention they gave to the love of God. Indeed, for Herbert man's sinfulness and God's love were twinned: the very consciousness of the former invariably led him to a consideration of the latter and intensified the poet's wonder at its vastness. In contrast, Thomas made few references to divine love and those few stress its fierceness. In reviewing a collection of essays about Thomas, Wolford Gealy observed, "In R. S. there is very little of Love's bidding to His feast and nowhere, it appears, does the bard sit down and eat his meat" (*New Welsh Review*, Winter 1991–1992, p. 27). Gealy's conscious invocation of Herbert's "Love (III)" which begins "Love bade me welcome …" and concludes "So I did sit and eat," sharply delineates Thomas's divergence from Herbert.

1.

In commenting on the structure of *The Temple*, I have said little about the long first section "The Church-porch," seventy-seven sestets which are very didactic in tone, being a series of admonitions against those things which inhibit us from proceeding on the Christian journey. Hutchinson described it as preparation for reading the main body of the poems: if the whole work may indeed be regarded as a description of that journey, "The Church-porch" is the necessary stage of purgation that precedes a pilgrimage. It concludes: "If thou do ill; the joy fades, not the pains: / If well, the pain doth fade, the joy remains." As we enter "The Church," the voice shifts from admonitory to confessional. The narrator proclaims his unworthiness ("A broken ALTAR, Lord, thy servant reares, / Made of a heart, and cemented with teares…," "The Altar") and acknowledges the great sacrifice of the Crucified Jesus ("The Sacrifice")—and in the reading the confession becomes our own. Those are the recurrent themes of his work, and Herbert quickly linked them.

The third poem in the opening sequence is "Thanksgiving." The recurrent refrain of "The Sacrifice" ("Was ever grief like mine"), intensified in the closing variation ("Never was grief like mine"), elicits the opening acclamation, "Oh King of grief! (a title strange, yet true, / To thee of all kings onely due)." But the poem is not merely a prayer of thanksgiving, it is also, even more so, a plaintive cry: What can I possibly do to give proper thanks? And the poem ends, "Then for thy passion—I will do for that—/ Alas, my God, I know not what." The spiritual life is the struggle to shape an answer.

> Philosophers have measur'd mountains,
> Fathom'd the depths of seas, of states, and kings,
> Walk'd with a staffe to heav'n, and traced fountains:
>   But there are two vast, spacious things,
> The which to measure it doth more behove:
> Yet few there are that sound them; Sinne and Love.
>
> Who would know Sinne, let him repair
> Unto Mount Olivet; there shall he see
> A man so wrung with pains, that all his hair,
>   His skinne, his garments bloudie be.
> Sinne is that presse and vice, which forceth pain
> To hunt his cruell food through ev'ry vein.
>
> Who knows not Love, let him assay
> And taste that juice, which on the crosse a pike
> Did set again abroach; then let him say
>   If ever he did taste the like.
> Love is that liquor sweet and most divine,
> Which my God feels as bloud, but I, as wine,
>   —"The Agonie"

If one would know the nature of sin look to the suffering that was required to cleanse it, the passion of Christ. If one would know the nature of love look to what God has given. Herbert's poem is a striking gloss on

John 3:16: "For God so loved the world, that he gave his only-begotten Son, that whosoever believeth in him should not perish, but have everlasting life." And time and again in his poetry, and in his spiritual struggles, Herbert confronted the magnitude of that love and what response it required.

In *The Temple* Herbert included three poems entitled "Love," the first two are paired relatively early in the manuscript and the third concludes it. (Thomas includes all three in his selection of Herbert's verse.) Appropriately, "Love (I)" and "Love (II)" are presented together because they have a common theme, a contrast between Love and what passes for love among humankind.

> Immortal Love, author of this great frame,
>> Sprung from that beautie which can never fade;
>> How hath man parcel'd out thy glorious name,
> And thrown it on that dust which thou hast made,
> While mortall love doth all the title gain!
>> —"Love (I)," ll. 1–5

> Immortall Heat, O let thy greater flame
>> Attract the lesser to it: let those fires,
>> Which shall consume the world, first make it tame;
> And kindle in our hearts such true desires,
> As may consume our lusts, and make thee way.
>> —"Love (II)," ll. 1–5

The first poem provides a brief for Herbert's own vocation as a poet and chides the love poets for aiming too low. "Wit fancies beautie, beautie raiseth wit" and they prattle about "mortall love" while forgetting the source of all love — and the sure sign of that love which exceeds all others, the Cross. Herbert thus set himself the task of singing the praises of God: not that he was more worthy to do so than others, but that the gift of poesy which he had received itself required him to sing despite his own unworthiness. Man "is a brittle crazie glass," but God is able to shine through him for the good of others.

Virtually all the English poetry we have from Herbert's hand is religious poetry, and is about the issues of the relationship between God and man. Unlike his mother's great friend, John Donne, Herbert did not first produce a body of secular poetry and then turn to holy things. And unlike Thomas he did not produce (or at least did not keep) any poems which praise the love of husband and wife. In "Love (I)" he does not even write of "mortall love" as if it were a foreshadowing or echo of Divine Love.

Rather it is purely mundane, even trivial: "Onely a skarf or glove / Doth warm our hands, and make them write of love."

Every indication is that Herbert loved his wife Jane (and Walton's negative comments about her may be dismissed). Even so, in *A Priest to the Temple*, Herbert noted:

> The Country Parson considering that Virginity is a higher state than Matrimony, and that the Ministry requires the highest and best things, is rather unmarried, then marryed. But yet as the temper of his body may be, or as the temper of his Parish may be, where he may have occasion to converse with women, and that among suspicious men, *and other like circumstances considered*, he is rather married than unmarried. Let him communicate the thing often by prayer unto God, and as his grace shall direct him, so let him proceed.

He went on to say:

> If he be marryed, the choyce of his wife was made rather by his eare, then by his eye; his judgment, not his affection found out a fit wife for him, whose humble, and liberall disposition he preferred before beauty, riches, or honour.

Nothing there that is the stuff of romance.

"Love (II)" does suggest that "mortall love" may be a prelude to loving God, but, if so, it is because God's own love draws to it the lesser fire, transforming it:

> Then shall our hearts pant thee; then shall our brain
> All her invention on thine Altar lay,
> And there in hymnes send back thy fire again:
> Our eies shall see thee, which before saw dust....

Herbert, however, was not simply referring to the love between man and woman. He was speaking of all human desires and affections and lusts: for knowledge, for honor, for power, for money, for pleasure. These must be subdued, scorched by the Immortal Heat of God's great love. Yet as he made clear in the immediately following poem, "The Temper (I)," this is not the doing of a single moment, but of an ongoing struggle to accept that love.

> How should I praise thee, Lord! how should my rymes
>   Gladly engrave thy love in steel,
>   If what my soul doth feel sometimes
>   My soul might ever feel!

Again, the spiritual life is the struggle of finite beings to grasp some sense of God's love and to incline their hearts to it. Not surprisingly, therefore, Herbert concluded the central portion of his manuscript with "Love (III)":

> Love bade me welcome: yet my soul drew back,
> Guiltie of dust and sinne.
> But quick-ey'd Love, observing me grow slack
> From my first entrance in,
> Drew nearer to me, sweetly questioning,
> If I lack'd anything.
>
> A guest, I answer'd, worthy to be here:
> Love said, You shall be he.
> I the unkinde, ungratefull? Ah my deare,
> I cannot look on thee.
> Love took my hand, and smiling did reply,
> Who made the eyes but I?
>
> Truth Lord, but I have marr'd them: let my shame
> Go where it doth deserve.
> And know you not, sayes Love, who bore the blame?
> My deare, then I will serve.
> You must sit down, sayes Love, and taste my meat;
> So I did sit and eat.

This poem reverberates with all the themes and images which inspired and informed his work: his hesitations ("My soul drew back"), his sense of unworthiness ("I cannot look on thee"), God's persistent, even insistent, love ("You must sit down"), the Crucifixion ("Who bore the blame?"), the Eucharist ("Taste my meat"), and finally submission ("So I did sit and eat"). The form is not a prayer or a song of praise, but a dialogue, the summation, in effect, of all the pushings and pullings, the to-ings and fro-ings, of which his spiritual life consisted—and which characterize the universal experience of the Christian pilgrimage. In the end Herbert recognized, not only that God loves, but that God is Love and that in him is perfect freedom.

James Boyd White calls "Love (III)" Herbert's greatest poem, not merely because of the eloquence of its eighteen lines, but because it forms the perfect coda to the whole body of Herbert's poetry. It is difficult to quarrel with that assessment, for it is the final, fulsome echo of a man who has "heard one calling, *Child!*" and has "reply'd, *My Lord.*"

2.

The ways in which Thomas usually described his poetic enterprise (e.g., "Primarily I'm trying to find out what it means to use the word 'God' in the late twentieth century") make his quest seem narrowly rational, almost academic, affording very little room for admitting the kind of experiences with God that Herbert articulated, God as Infinite Love. But Thomas was not a scientific rationalist, nor was he a theologian in the academic sense: he was a poet and a priest who labored among the people. In "Neb" he described how he struggled, at first unconsciously, with the tensions between the beauty of the land and the hard lot of the people who scratched to earn a living from it, between the call to nurture the spirit and the grinding realities of his parishioners' daily lives. From those tensions came poetry, the crisp, sharp-edged poems such as "The Peasant" or "On the Farm" that unsentimentally depict rural Wales and its people, yet even they led toward the poems that gave voice to the enduring questions of faith.

> There was Dai Puw. He was no good.
> They put him into the fields to dock swedes,
> And took the knife from him, when he came home
> At late evening with a grin
> Like the slash of a knife on his face.
>
> There was Llew Puw. He was no good.
> Every evening after the ploughing
> With the big tractor he would sit in his chair,
> And stare into the tangled fire garden,
> Opening his slow lips like a snail.
>
> There was Huw Puw, too. What shall I say?
> I have heard him whistling in the hedges
> On and on, as though winter
> Would never again leave those fields,
> And all the trees were deformed.
>
> And lastly there was the girl:
> Beauty under some spell of the beast.
> Her pale face was the lantern
> By which they read in life's dark book
> The shrill sentence: God is love.
>   —"On the Farm," *The Bread of Truth*

As he argued in the introduction to *The Penguin Book of Religious Verse*, invoking Coleridge, it is the creative imagination that allows us to approach God most nearly, which is not to say, however, that it carries us to the heart of truth.

> ... The main fact in the religious consciousness of western man is the Judeo-Christian revelation. The need for revelation at all suggests an ultimate reality beyond human attainment, the *mysterium tremendum et fascinans*. And here surely is common ground between religion and poetry.... The presentation of religious experience in the most inspired language is poetry. This is not a definition of poetry, but a description of how the communication of religious experience best operates [p. 9].

"Best" not "perfect," for our creative imagination, no less than our reason, is flawed and the poet lives "in uncertainties, mysteries, doubts."

Certainly, Thomas's ability to live and write in such a condition was expressed forcefully in the title of his last collection, *No Truce with the Furies*. That collection begins with the poem "Geriatric":

What god is proud
    of this garden
of dead flowers, this underwater
    grotto of humanity,
where limbs wave in invisible
    currents, faces drooping
on dry stalks, voices clawing
    in a last desperate effort
to retain hold? Despite withered
    petals, I recognize
the species: Charcot, Meniere,
    Alzheimer. There are no gardeners
here, caretakers only
    of reason overgrown
by confusion, This body once,
    when it was in bud,
opened to love's kisses. These eyes
    cloudy with rheum,
were clear pebbles that love's rivulet
    hurried over. Is this
the best Rabbi Ben Ezra
    promised? I come away
comforting myself, as I can,

> that there is another
> garden, all dew and fragrance,
>   and that these are the brambles
> about it we are caught in,
>   a sacrifice prepared
> by a torn god to a love fiercer
>   than we can understand.

While this poem does not occupy the deliberately chosen ultimate place in the whole body of Thomas's work which "Love (III)" does in Herbert's *The Temple*, its position is nonetheless significant. It defines the voice, sets the direction, and frames the themes of whatever is to come. There will be no truce with the furies of uncertainties, mysteries, doubts; there will be no surrender to the temptation to wrap himself in the emperor's clothes of fact and reason.

In the face of the hard realities of aging, all the dyings—of dreams, desires, clarity of mind—attendant to growing old, he will comfort himself as he can, as best he can, with the promise of another garden which that "love fiercer than we can understand" has prepared. The tenuous, yet tenacious, character of this comfort reiterates a quality that runs through Thomas's poetry, especially of the last decade. One recalls the concluding poem of the probing, passionate *Counterpoint* (1990):

> I think that maybe
> I will be a little surer
> of being a little nearer.
> That's all. Eternity
> is in the understanding
> that that little is more than enough.

Strikingly also, the word "love" appears three times in "Geriatric," not a common occurrence in Thomas's verse. The first two times (ll. 17, 19) it refers to human love, the love of man and woman. While the usage suggests the transitory nature of that love, it also emphasizes the centrality of it for the human experience. The acts and looks of love bind us to others, bridge our isolation. One hardly thinks of Thomas as a love poet, but over the long years of his writing career, he produced a number of truly and profoundly beautiful poems inspired by his wife, Elsi, perhaps none lovelier than one written after her death in 1991.

We met
    under a shower
of bird-notes.
      Fifty years passed,
love's moment
    in a world in
servitude to time.
      She was young;
I kissed with my eyes
    closed and opened
them on her wrinkles.
      'Come,' said death,
choosing her as his
    partner for
the last dance. And she,
    who in life
had done everything
    with a bird's grace,
opened her bill now
    for the shedding
of one sigh no
    heavier than a feather.
                —"A Marriage"

This appears close to the end of his collection *Mass for Hard Times* (1992), but also is the last poem — obviously a late addition — in the major edition of his works, *Collected Poems, 1945–1990* (1993). Thomas then, like Herbert, ended with a song of love, albeit human love.

Thomas made no effort to portray that love as proleptic to or preparatory for the love of God. In "Geriatric" the third reference to love (l. 29) is to God's love, which is "fiercer than we can understand." Our own loves do not help us to grasp the scope and nature of it.

Twenty-one of the sixty-seven poems in *No Truce with the Furies* refer to love, not quite half in the sense of human love, the others invoking it as a force apart, sometimes directive or creative. He never quite says "God is Love" or "Love is God" except in the poem "Blind Noel" which concludes:

Love knocks with such frosted fingers.
I look out. In the shadow
of so vast a God I shiver, unable
to detect the child for the whiteness.

R. S. Thomas and M. E. Eldridge on their wedding day. Bala, July 1940 (courtesy Gwydion Thomas).

So, indeed, Thomas never "sits and eats," rather he shivers.

It is in this collection that Thomas described his alienation from Herbert — and Thomas Traherne, John Donne, and Gerard Manley Hopkins:

> Easier for them, God
> only at the beginning
> of his recession. Blandish him,
> said the times and they did so,
> Herbert, Traherne, walking
> in a garden not yet
> polluted. Music in Donne's
> mind was still polyphonic.
>
> The corners of the spirit waiting
> to be developed, Hopkins
> renewed the endearments
> taming the lion-like presence
> lying against him. What
> happened? Suddenly he was
> gone, leaving love guttering
> in his withdrawal. And scenting
> disaster, as flies are attracted
> to a carcase, far down
> in the subconscious the ghouls
> and the demons we thought
> we had buried for ever resurrected.
> — "Resurrections"

Parenthetically, the phrase in l. 11, "renewed the endearments," reminds us of Thomas's discomfort with Herbert's mode of address to God.

"In the shadow / of so vast a God," Thomas shivered, but he did not give way. He would not settle for less than the promise of that fierce love:

> In a universe
> that is expanding our theologies
> have contracted. We reduce
> the God-man to the human, the human
> to the machine, watching it demolish
> forests faster than we can grow even
> one tree of faith for our Saviour
> to come down from.
> — "How?"

With his death in September, 2000, this poem, the last of six published together in 1997, seems a valedictory. If so, it is an appropriate one, for as always he pressed forward with his questions. "How do we sing the Lord's song" in times such as ours? Not, he declared, by changing the questions so we can more easily answer them. *The* question remains, as it always has been: the Cross, that sign of a "love fiercer than we can understand."

3.

Herbert and Thomas were both poets of the Cross. For Herbert, the Cross was the most dramatic sign of God's love. As we have seen, "The Church" begins with a poem "The Altar" and immediately after it comes "The Sacrifice," by far the longest poem in the manuscript (252 lines). Rosamund Tuve, in her analysis of "Sacrifice," observed that in Herbert we find a series of contrasts between man's action towards God and God's action towards man, and above all between man's conception of the relationship between Creator and creature and the actuality of that relationship. (*A Reading of George Herbert*, p. 49.)

This was not mere abstraction, a general description of the human condition, it was deeply particular and personal, which is what gives Herbert's poetry its universal force. Richard Baxter (1615–1691), one of the most appealing figures of seventeenth-century English Puritanism, said of him, "Herbert speaks to God like a man that really believeth in God and whose business in the world is most with God, heart-work and heaven-work make up his book." Herbert's poetry and life were infused with his consuming emphasis on Divine Love. Indeed, the Love of God is the central theme in his poetry, around which spiral accounts of man's recurring struggle to respond adequately to it.

For Herbert himself the problem was always his own unfitness, his sense that he was unworthy to preach that eternal word. There were times that he tried to turn away; there were times that he suffered the silence of God. Those thrashings about and agonies were, in a sense, two sides of the same coin, for Herbert would say with Augustine that God is not far from us, even when we are far from him. What we experience as God's silence is only our own deafness, the result of the clanking of the chains of our mortality. In the end, however, he gave way before the weight of that glory which proclaimed: "God so loved the world, that he gave his only-begotten son to the end that all that believe in him should not perish, but have everlasting life" (John 3:16). There is then a resolution in Herbert's story, a coming to rest, when he finally says he abides in God's love.

For Thomas there was no such rest. To him our experience of God is more with his silence, his absence evokes his presence. Thus it is difficult to talk easily, familiarly, about God's love. And because we cannot talk about it easily, the Cross looms more starkly over our works and days. Thomas says he is "trying to find out what it means to use the word 'God'" in our times. It is critical to understand the issue: it is not God, but the word 'God' and how we use it that is at issue. In an interview in 1981 he noted "What I'm tilting at is not God, but the ideas of God" ("R. S. Thomas Talks with J. B. Lethbridge," *The Anglo-Welsh Review*, 74 [1983], p. 40). We are always attempting to pin down God, to define him, but words always fall short. As C. S. Lewis declares, "My idea of God is not a divine idea. It has to be shattered time after time. He himself shatters it" (*A Grief Observed*, p. 52). The problem, however, is not simply the insufficiency of language, but our failure to recognize the insufficiency, to appreciate the ultimate mystery of God's transcendence. We are forever saying that what was said about God was imperfect, conditioned by the prevailing world-view, but now we have got it right. While that is the particular addiction of theologians, it is true as well of all our attempts to define God, even to say "God is Love." The way we use that phrase in our day is often fatu-ous, rather than poetic. Poetic language, which is the best we have, is sug-gestive, metaphorical, partial, not definitive, but also not simply warm and fuzzy. It leads us onward for we always must be at the labor.

> The waves run up the shore
> and fall back. I run
> up the approaches of God
> and fall back. The breakers return
> reaching a little further,
> gnawing away at the main land.
> They have done this thousands
> of years, exposing little by little
> the rock under the soil's face.
> I must imitate them only
> in my return to the assault,
> not in their violence. Dashing
> my prayers at him will achieve
> little other than the exposure
> of the rock under his surface.
> My returns must be made
> on my knees. Let despair be known
> as my ebb-tide; but let prayer
> have its springs, too, brimming,

disarming him; discovering somewhere
among his fissures deposits of mercy
where trust may take root and grow.
                    "Tidal," *Mass for Hard Times*

Thomas's struggle is less with a sense of unworthiness than it is with the ravages of doubt. Like that other Thomas, R. S. cried, "Lord, I believe, help thou my unbelief." But in his poetry, no less than in Herbert's, we find the contrasts "between man's action towards God and God's action towards man, and above all between man's conception of the relationship between Creator and creature and the actuality of that relationship." The central symbol of that relationship remains the Cross. What can we make of it? Can this be Love?

IX

"Oh What a Thing Is Man!"

Among the historical phenomena which produced or comprise "the discoveries and changes which have come about in the human intellect" from the seventeenth to the end of the twentieth centuries and which therefore separate Thomas from Herbert, the chief are the Scientific Revolution and the Age of Enlightenment. Yet, one might also venture to say that together the two poets form parentheses around those phenomena. Herbert lived as the Scientific Revolution was beginning, the age of Francis Bacon and Galileo, while Thomas's life spanned the twentieth century that saw the doctrines of the Enlightenment shattered by the horrors of the Holocaust, nuclear weapons and repeated incidents of ethnic cleansing. Given the demonstrated imperfections of human reason, science and technology have proven to be double-edged swords. And even as we know more, we have come to recognize that we know less of what there is to know. From opposite sides of the chasm, as it were, Herbert and Thomas challenged — and continue to challenge — the assumptions and expectations of those centuries.

1.

Classic Anglicanism as exemplified in the writings of Richard Hooker posits the notion that the elements that support and sustain the faith are Scripture, Tradition and Reason. Often this notion is characterized as a "three-legged stool," which suggests a balance and equivalency among them. That characterization begs the question of the particular dynamic among elements that, after all, are themselves different orders of things. It is enough to know that Hooker and others assigned a far more important role to human reason than did many English Protestants, particularly the Puritans for whom man's depravity so sullied his reason that it could contribute nothing to his salvation; all was dependent on saving grace.

Herbert appears to be closer to the Puritan view on this than to Hooker's. One has only to read the "Affliction" poems, or any number of others, to recognize that Herbert put small store in his own ability, if not man's generally, to help himself. In "The Pearl" he began by declaring:

> I know the wayes of Learning; both the head
> And pipes that feed the presse, and make it run;
> What reason hath from nature borrowed,
> Or of it self, like a good huswife, spunne
> In laws and policies....

But after declaring as well his grasp of "the wayes of Honour" and "the wayes of Pleasure," he concluded:

> Yet through these labyrinths, not my groveling wit,
> But thy silk twist let down from heav'n to me,
> Did both conduct and teach me, how by it
> > To climbe to thee.

Even with a distinguished academic record at Westminster School and Trinity College, Cambridge, Herbert stressed holiness rather than knowledge as the proper goal of life. Significantly, in the chapter entitled "The Parson's Library" in *The Country Parson*, he mentioned no books at all. Rather he stated emphatically, "The Country Parson's Library is a holy Life: for besides the blessing that that brings upon it, there being a promise, that if the Kingdom of God be first sought, all other things shall be added, even it selfe is a Sermon" (*Works*, p. 278).

Yet, if it be God's "silk twist" let down from heaven that brings man to salvation, there still remains the fact that man must be taught to use it to climb to Him. Herbert clearly avowed the limits of human reason, as in "Giddinesse":

> He builds a house, which quickly down must go,
> > As if a whirlwinde blew
> And crusht the building: and it's partly true,
> > His minde is so.

The structures we build with our minds, the concepts by which we try to order the world around us, are ever being buffeted and battered. But he did not deny that reason too is a gift from God. It is what distinguishes man from the beasts of the field and the birds of the air, making him little less than the angels.

> To this life things of sense
> Make their pretence:
> In th' other Angels have a right by birth:
> Man ties them both alone,
> And makes them one,
> With the one hand touching heav'n, with th' other earth.
> —"Man's Medley"

The respect he had for the possibilities of human intellect is seen in his relationship with Francis Bacon. Bacon was himself a graduate of Trinity College, Cambridge, maintained close contact with the University, and, not surprisingly given Bacon's stature as Chancellor of England the University reciprocated the interest. Furthermore, he was a frequent visitor to Danvers House, home of Herbert's mother and stepfather, Sir John Danvers. When Bacon published his *Novum Organum* (1620) in which he made the case for inductive reasoning, the basis of the scientific method, he presented a copy to Cambridge and Herbert, in his role as Public Orator, wrote the letter of appreciation to Bacon. Of course, such letters by definition were fulsome, but Herbert had not only read, understood and appreciated Bacon's work, he had helped to translate the manuscript from English into Latin. Additionally, Herbert wrote three Latin poems in which he praised Bacon's intellectual ability and the substance of his work. In one he wrote: "While you give aid to us who live today / By means of your position, to those who live tomorrow / By virtue of your book, all times praise you" (McCloskey and Murphy, *The Latin Poetry of George Herbert*, p. 167). The longest of these poems was a veritable catalogue of encomiums, Herbert calling Bacon "The instigator of research, archpriest / of truth, lord of the inductive method ..., Savior of science ..., Minister of light ..., Sense and reason's miraculous / Discriminator ..., Atlas of Nature," to cite but a few.

Bacon's brilliant public career ended in disgrace and he spent time confined in the Tower of London, but the connection with Herbert persisted. One of Bacon's final writing efforts was a versification of the psalms, a work he dedicated to "his very good friend, George Herbert." And when Bacon died in 1626 Herbert was one of few Cambridge men who contributed to the memorial volume printed in his honor, penning an eloquent six-line Latin poem.

Most of this occurred before Herbert himself had eschewed the "wayes of learning,... of Honour,... of Pleasure." Perhaps Bacon's fall from grace influenced Herbert's own decision to turn away from any court ambitions. Doubtless he knew of the prayer which Bacon had written asking God's forgiveness for wasting his talents on the wrong endeavors. Even so, Herbert's decision not to rely on his own "groveling wit" cannot be regarded as a total rejection of reason: man does not serve his Creator by rejecting reason, but by aligning it with God's will. For all his breast-beating and self-deprecation, Herbert also asserted in his poem "Man,"

> My God I heard this day,
> That none doth build a stately habitation,
> But he that means to dwell therein.
> What house more stately hath there been,
> Or can be, then is Man? to whose creation
> All things are in decay.
>
> For Man is ev'ry thing,
> And more: He is a tree, yet beares more fruit;
> A beast, yet is, or should be more:
> Reason and speech we onely bring.
> Parrats may thank us, if they are not mute,
> They go upon the score.

This "hymn to man," as it were, comes immediately after "The Pearl" and "Affliction (IV)," thus balancing their affirmations, as they balance it. As noted before, this is one of Herbert's qualities, as it is one of Thomas's. Recognizing the limits of language, he did not write a definitive poem. *The Temple* is a whole, structured to give an account, rather than a collection of discrete entities that stand by themselves, though we may profit from reading individual ones.

In *The Country Parson* Herbert delineated the responsibilities of the priest for his people. Clearly, he regarded it as essential for the priest to use his intelligence and reason in dealing with them — always beginning, of course, with the humble prayer that he might use them to serve God, not himself. An apt illustration of this is Chapter XXI, "The Parson catechizing." He stressed that catechizing is the best means of carrying out his responsibilities. He began, of course, with the standard catechetical form, but Herbert went beyond mere recitation. By developing the art of questioning, the parson can move his people beyond the mere parroting of the catechism to a deeper sense of the faith. He recommended reading some of Plato's dialogues as a means of learning the necessary skill. That skill involves having a clear understanding of the "aim and mark" of the whole discourse before asking the first question, knowing how to frame each question, and finally knowing how to use illustrations that draw on the knowledge of the one questioned to bring him to understand. He noted that at sermons or prayers men's attention may wander, but when being questioned "he must discover what he is."

Likewise, in Chapter XXIV, "The Parson arguing," he described how the parson should approach any parishioners who hold "strange Doctrines." He called for argument without contention, but one based on a rational analysis of the "main foundation, and pillar of their cause" so that he might approach them wisely. "Reason and speech" are the instruments by which the parson brings his people to the point at which that "peace which passeth all understanding" can reach and raise them.

If it was God's "silk twist" let down to him that would lift him, Herbert nonetheless did not abandon the "wayes of learning." Rather he subordinated them to the task of articulating God's will. In that regard the classical training which he received served him well. It served well in his poetry, too. Typical of the "metaphysical" poets, Herbert's imagery and allusions reflected the range of his learning, including science. I have already noted his connection with Francis Bacon. Given his long connection with Cambridge, he may well have known something of Galileo's observations. Certainly, of the sciences, astronomy is the one of which he seemed the most aware, perhaps because of his fondness for star images— or does that fondness derive from his interest in astronomy? Interestingly, also, he was dismissive of the classical theory of celestial spheres. His poem "Divinitie" opens

> As men, for fear the starres should sleep and nod,
>   And trip at night, have spheres suppli'd;
> As if a starre were duller than a clod,
>   Which knows his way without a guide:

And concluded:

> Then burn thy Epicycles, foolish man;
>   Break all thy spheres, and save thy head.
> Faith needs no staffe of flesh, but stoutly can
>   To heav'n alone both go, and leade.

The theories of classical astronomy, then, were not divine laws governing the universe, but the musings of man, his presumptive efforts to explain, another of his houses which "down must go." (One also sees here the influence of Bacon's critique of Aristotle.)

Herbert was not arguing, of course, for Galileo, but against the vanity of man who though "He did not heav'n and earth create, / Yet studies them, not him by whom they be" ("Mattens"). Thus in "Vanitie (I)", Herbert chided the efforts of astronomers who study the stars and chemists who analyze matter with the query "What hath not man sought out and found, / But his deare God?" Again, however, it was not reason or the scientific method that he deplored, but the misuse of them, seeing them as ends in themselves. As he said in "Mattens,"

> Teach me thy love to know;
> That this new light, which now I see,
> May both the work and workman show:
> Then by a sunne-beam I will climbe to thee.

2.

In his autobiographical writings, "Neb" and *The Echoes Return Slow*, Thomas referred slightingly to his formal education at University College, Bangor, and at seminary in Llandaff, blaming himself as much as, if not more than, the institutions, noting his immaturity. In the latter work he observed:

> He rationed his intake
> of knowledge. On fine days
> with the mountains leaning
> over him to whisper
>
> there were other picnics
> beside the musty sandwiches
> in the library. Foolish
> youth, doing only
>
> enough work to enable
> him to answer set
> questions ...

But if he lacked the rich formal education that Herbert received at Westminster School and Trinity, Cambridge, Thomas compensated by wide and deep reading in philosophy and science as well as literature. His poetry, especially from the late 1960s on, reflects the breadth of his self-education with both specific references to and images drawn from philosophy, science and technology.

However, even though he often described his purposes in terms that suggest they are rationalistic, he was stubbornly skeptical about human reason as well as about the human consequences of science and technology. In "Synopsis" (*Frequencies*, 1978) he summed up the history of philosophy thusly:

> Plato offered us little
> the Aristotelians did not
> take back. Later Spinoza
> rationalised our approach;
> we were taught that love
> is an intellectual mode
> of our being. Yet Hume questioned
> the very existence of lover
> or loved. The self he left us
> with was what Kant
> failed to transcend or Hegel
> to dissolve: that grey subject
> of dread that Soren Kierkegaard
> depicted crossing its thousands
> of fathoms; the beast that rages
> through history; that presides smiling
> at the councils of the positivists.

If there was a philosopher to whom Thomas was particularly drawn, it was Kierkegaard. He made various references to him in his poetry, nowhere more fully and eloquently than in *No Truce with the Furies*. In a poem simply entitled "S. K." Thomas outlined the biography of the Dane in a way that evokes the essential qualities of his thought — and explains his appeal, at least to Thomas.

> … He learned
> his anonymity from God himself,
>
> leaving his readers, as God
> leaves the reader in life's
>
> book to grope for the meaning
> that will be quicksilver in the hand.

What Thomas found in Kierkegaard was not a teacher, but a companion on the way with whom he shared a sense of both the possibilities and the limits of human reason and language. Kierkegaard does not offer a meticulous road map, but sudden illuminations, like flares in the night, that allow the searcher to proceed yet further on his journey, to say "I think that maybe / I will be a little surer / of being a little nearer." But there is never certainty. Thomas concluded "S. K." thusly:

> How do we know his study
> was not the garden
> over again, where his mind
> was the serpent, insinuator
> of the heresy of the self
> as God? The difficulty
> with prayer is the exchange
> of places between I and thou,
> with silence as the answer
> to an imagined request.
> Is this the price genius
> must pay, that from an emphasis
> on the subjective only
> soliloquy remains? Is prayer
> not a glass that, beginning
> in obscurity as his books
> do, the longer we stare
> into the clearer becomes
> the reflection of a countenance
> in it other than our own?

To understand the limits of reason is not to deny reason, but to grasp a truth which, until recently, has been eclipsed in Western thought, that reason is only one way of knowing. Let us look again at Thomas's description of his purpose: "Primarily I'm trying to find out what it means to use the word 'God' in the late twentieth century with all the discoveries and changes which have come about in the human intellect." He was not simply iterating a rationalistic enterprise. He understood that the search for meaning requires us to use all the means we have at hand, including the ways of reason. He did not retreat from the Enlightenment and the Scientific Revolution, but went beyond them and he found justification for his effort in the newest developments in physics as well as in ancient wisdom.

Lecturing at the University College, Swansea, in 1985, Thomas observed,

> The West has been under the thumb of reason for a very long time. Because of this we divide everything into A and not-A. Nothing can be A and not-A at the same time. However, contemporary physics contradicts this by showing how matter is both a wave and a particle at the same time, and by describing the strange behaviour of one of the elements of life, the electron. We are gradually beginning to see how the scientific mind works. Some of the most abstruse and complex problems of nature have been solved, not by means of a process of reasoning, but as a result of a sudden intuition which was closer to the vision of an artist or a saint than anything else. (See his poem "Suddenly.") This explains the increasing interest in Zen Buddhism, a technique which does its best to wean the mind away from its traditional rational mode to understand things by behaving in an extremely whimsical and laughable way at times.
>
> —"Unity"

This is not a casual observation. Thomas kept abreast of contemporary scientific developments and wove what he had learned into his art. Not that he wrote poems about science, but he used the images of science (and technology), used them as well metaphorically, because they form a part of the language of our times. Again, in *No Truce with the Furies*, he said:

> With the cathedrals thundering
> at him, history proving
> him the two-faced god, there were
> the few who waited on him
> in the small hours, undaunted
> by the absence of an echo
> to their Amens. Physics' suggestion
> is they were not wrong. Reality
> is composed of waves and particles
> coming at us as the Janus-faced
> chooses. We must not despair.
> The invisible is yet susceptible
> of being inferred. To pray, perhaps, is
> to have a part in an infinitesimal deflection.
> —"Nuance"

Wave theory, particle theory, uncertainty principle, chaos theory, gene mutation, evolution: all these and more find their way into Thomas's verse, working and contending with more traditional poetic images and meta-phors drawn from nature, music, art, literature. The usage is dazzling and sometimes cacophonous, but always provocative. The final poem in *Mass for Hard Times*, "Sonata in X," vividly illustrates these qualities. In many respects it seems an epitome of Thomas's efforts to find language to express the themes, the ideas, the questions he has so long probed. Some may find the range too broad. It is certainly not a minimalist sonata and may very well require a deep reading of all the previous poems in the collection before one can detect the melodic line of thought beneath apparent dis-sonance.

The dissonance itself becomes a metaphor for the world in which we live, but Thomas was not content to leave it at that, to accept the notion that we are isolated from one another, living fragmented lives. The speech quoted above is entitled "Unity." In it he dealt with the ideas of the unity of being, of humankind and of Wales, finally affirming each. We find the same commitment to struggle on, to use the imperfect instruments of mind and language whether poetic or scientific, for both are finally metaphorical, in the poetry he composed in his old age.

> ... Winged God
> approve that in a world
> that has appropriated flight
> to itself there are still people
> like us, who believe
> in the ability of the heart
> to migrate, if only momentarily
> between the quotidian and the sublime.
> —"Bird Watching," *No Truce with the Furies*

3.

In a general sense one can argue that Herbert and Thomas had similar attitudes toward reason and science. Both recognized reason as a central aspect of human nature, but understood its limits and imperfections. Both were knowledgeable about the scientific learning of their day and used that knowledge as a source of metaphor — Thomas more readily and frequently. But to say this is only to speak at a superficial level, for there is a qualitative difference in their approach to these oft-twinned phenomena. And the difference is rooted in the fact that they stand on two sides of the great gulf which the Enlightenment and the Scientific Revolution produced, "all the discoveries and changes which have come about in the human intellect."

If Herbert acknowledged reason as a gift of God, he had little confidence that it could carry man very far toward God. As he makes clear in "Giddinesse" reason is as much a source of man's errors as of his knowledge. And finally it is not his "groveling wit," but God's unimaginable love that brings the heart's peace. Even the elegant hymn to man ("Man") concludes,

> Since then, my God, thou hast
> So brave a palace built; O dwell in it,
> That it may dwell with thee at last!
> Till then, afford us so much wit;
> That, as the world serves us, we may serve thee,
> And both thy servants be.

If Thomas acknowledged that human reason is fundamentally flawed, he nonetheless saw it as the primary — though not the only — instrument we have to discern meaning. The puerile confidence of the Age of Reason has foundered, but we go on, chastened, yet enduring.

> Man, two
> million years at
> his back — parvenu.
>
> Kestrel,
> older, arrested
> permanently in its ascent.
>
> Rock of
> no age, its hundred-weights
> fortuitously poised.
>
> Now! Man,
> car, rock in the high
> pass keeping an appointment.
>
> Witness?
> The kestrel in the sky
> burning, but not to tell.
> —"Sonata in X"

If Herbert was open to the ideas of the new science, it was only a peripheral interest to him, at best another means of glorifying the God of

Creation. It was too early yet to believe science could open the secrets of the universe. If Thomas knew too much about how humankind has used science for ill and saw the optimistic promises of the belief in human progress fade, he could still see in the new physics a hope that we might yet come to understand that proximate truth is what we have to live by.

In the end Herbert would say:

> Teach me, my God and King,
> In all things thee to see,
> And what I do in any thing,
> To do it as for thee:
>
> Not rudely, as a beast,
> To runne into an action;
> But still to make thee prepossest,
> And give it his perfection.
>
> A man that looks on glasse,
> On it may stay his eye;
> Or if he pleaseth, through it passe,
> And then the heav'n espie.
>
> All may of thee partake:
> Nothing can be so mean,
> Which with his tincture (for thy sake)
> Will not grow bright and clean.
>
> A servant with this clause
> Makes drudgerie divine:
> Who sweeps a room, as for thy laws,
> Makes that and th'action fine.
>
> This is the famous stone
> That turneth all to gold:
> For that which God doth touch and own
> Cannot for lesse be told.
> —"The Elixir"

Not only the thought, but the imagery as well is telling. Herbert lived in a time when alchemy was not yet disjoined from science and so he took metaphors from it as easily as from what we would call true science. All things might be used to praise God, for that is the proper end of all human activity.

Thomas ventured:

> I would still go there
> if only to await
> the once-in-a-lifetime
> opening of truth's flower;
>
> if only to escape
> such bought freedom, and live,
> prisoner of the keyless sea,
> on the mind's bread and water.
>   —"Island," *No Truce with the Furies*

Such is the place to which the Enlightenment and the Scientific Revolution have brought us.

X.

*Cross-pollination:
"Truth's Flower"*

"The once-in-a-lifetime / opening of truth's flower" of which Thomas speaks in "Island" brings to mind what is probably the most often praised and perhaps most thoroughly analyzed of Herbert's poems, "The Flower." It is certainly one of Herbert's poems that Thomas found "most satisfactory in itself." He included the full poem in both *A Choice of Herbert's Verse* and *The Penguin Book of Religious Verse*, and stanzas two, three and six in *The Botsford Book of Country Verse*. In the introduction to *A Choice...*, Thomas observed,

> In him there is often the medievalist's depreciation of this life, with a corresponding eagerness for the next.... But in order to refute any overriding sense of world-negation, it is necessary only to quote a line or two from such a poem as 'The Flower'....

This observation arose from Thomas's own keen attentiveness to the natural world so evident in his poetry. He has sometimes been referred to as a "nature mystic," and one has only to read poems like "Sea-Watching" and "Moorland" to grasp the sense of that designation. We would not so call Herbert and his use of images from nature is less frequent. But he too was a country parson and walked daily to Salisbury, past fields and streams, and woodlands, and savored what he saw and heard. He loved God's creation.

1.

In *The Country Parson*, Herbert asserted:

> The Country Parson is full of all knowledg. They say, it is an ill Mason that refuseth any stone: and there is no knowledg, but in a skilfull hand, serves either positively as it is, or else to illustrate

some other knowledge. He condescends even to the knowledge of tillage, and pastorage, and makes great use of them in teaching, because people by what they understand, are best led to what they understand not [p. 228].

This suggests that the parson's knowledge of the natural world is primarily functional, a way of explaining the faith to people whose daily lives are so dependent on that world. But, if this enables him to "illustrate some other [and greater] knowledge," it is because God is creator of all things, because all creatures great and small are emblematic of His creative power. In the poem "Longing," Herbert said,

> Indeed the world's thy book,
> Where all things have their leafe assign'd:
> Yet a meek look
> Hath interlin'd.
> Thy board is full, yet humble guests
> Finde nests.

Herbert pursued this idea at length in "Providence," one of the longest poems in "The Church." It is a poem which is at once a hymn to God the Creator and to His Creation, an affirmation of man's special place in the order of things, and a description of that order as a great chain of being. It also reiterates Herbert's sense of responsibility as a poet. In doing all this, the poem emphasizes the sacredness of the natural world.

> Thou art in small things great, not small in any:
> Thy even praise can neither rise, nor fall.
> Thou art in all things one, in each thing many:
> For thou art infinite in one and all.
>
> —ll. 41–44

Therefore, man is not the master of the world with all else merely subservient to him, to be used as he wills. Rather he is the "high priest," whose responsibility it is to articulate for all creation due praise.

> Wherefore, most sacred Spirit, I here present
> For me and all my fellows praise to thee:
> And just it is that I should pay the rent,
> Because the benefit accrues to me.
>
> —ll. 25–29

In all things we may find cause for acknowledging God's creative power: "Each creature hath a wisdome for his good." And there is in the world a divine economy:

> How harsh are thorns to pears! and yet they make
> A better hedge, and need lesse reparation.
> How smooth are silks compared with a stake,
> Or with a stone! yet make no good foundation.
>
> Sometimes thou dost divide thy gifts to man,
> Sometimes unite. The Indian nut alone
> Is clothing, meat and trencher, drink and can,
> Boat, cable, sail and needle, all in one.
> —ll. 131–138

And so for all things praise, from all things praise, and that is the work of man above all:

> But who hath praise enough? nay, who hath any?
> None can express thy works, but he that knows them:
> And none can know thy works, which are so many,
> And so complete, but onely he that owes them.
> —ll. 141–144

If, as Thomas remarked, Herbert often seems medieval with his emphasis on the world to come, that tendency is softened and transformed, by his deep regard for what God hath wrought in the Creation and his understanding of how man lives and moves and has his being in the midst of nature. That places on man an awesome burden, not only to praise God from whom all these gifts do flow, but for using them wisely, respectfully, sacredly — a responsibility that we have too often forgotten, to our sorrow.

2.

The early reading of Thomas typed him as a poet of rural Wales and certainly the preponderance of poems in *The Stones of the Field* and *An Acre of Land* lend themselves to that view. Even *The Minister* might be regarded as a description of rural life. But Thomas was never merely a rural or nature poet, any more than he has ceased to be a rural or nature poet as he has steadily confronted more directly the great questions of God and man. He observed in "The Making of a Poem" that "I happen to be a person brought up in the country, living in the country and loving the country, and I try to understand what the country means and what it means to live in it..." (*Selected Prose*, p. 90). Thus throughout his creative life he found nature/the country to be an abundant source of images as well as an object of pure wonder.

In addition to the selection of Herbert's verse and the anthology of religious verse, Thomas edited three other collections: *The Botsford Book of Country Verse* (1961), *Selected Poems of Edward Thomas* (1964), and *A Choice of Wordsworth's Verse*. His introductions to those collections are instructive.

He noted of *The Botsford Book...* that it "is mainly for young people," and goes on to say:

> ... it was by way of nature that I first came to poetry. I loved some of these poems because they expressed for me something of the environment in which I was brought up, the power and beauty of the sea, and the excitement and changeableness of the seasons.... The environment of the majority of our population today is that of science, technology and industry. The natural world is presented fitfully and transitorily on the television screen or during a short holiday. Yet nature was man's background for thousands of years; the seasons provided a lovely rhythm to his life and thought. The country is still linked dearly with us through childhood memories. My first hope, therefore, in compiling this anthology has been to re-awaken those memories. We know that the most important thing in life is ... to find something to love. And perhaps one of the wisest ways of setting about this is to begin with the near and familiar. It is in learning to love and to cherish our own little tree, or field or brook that we become fitted for wider and deeper affections [pp. 7–8].

Of Edward Thomas he observed:

> Those who are mindful of the vanishing features of the English country-side and anxious to preserve them, will find in Edward Thomas one who loved them as they do. But there are more lasting aspects of country living, the ever-changing moods of nature and weather, which can say deep things to the human spirit. Thomas knew those as well, and told of them in lines which still make their impact, even in this industrial-technological era ... [p. 14].

Of Wordsworth he wrote: "His poems were almost entirely about the environment in which he loved to dwell, although the tree of poetry which grew from this natural soil soared into the upper air of the spirit. Wordsworth is,... perhaps, the supreme poet of atmosphere.... Yet the inadequacy of the description of him as a nature poet is obvious" (*Selected Prose*, p. 94). All of those observations as readily apply to R. S. Thomas's own "nature" poems from as early as the elegantly simple "Cyclamen"

> They are white moths
> With wings
> Lifted
> Over a dark water
> In act to fly;
> Yet stayed
> By their frail images
> In its mahogany depths.
> —*The Stones of the Field*

to the much later "The Hummingbird Never Came"

> We waited,
> breath held, looks aimed,
> the garden as tempting
> as ever. Was there a lack
> of nectar within us?
> God, too? We
> are waiting. Is it
> for the same reason
> he delays? Sourness,
> the intellect's
>
> dried-up comb? Dust
> where there should be
> pollen? Come, Lord;
> though our heads hang
> the bird's rainbow is above us.
> —*Six Poems*

The poems, separated by a half-century in their composition, differ dramatically. The first is elegant in its simplicity, perhaps deceptively simple; the second is eloquent in its complexity, perhaps deceptively complex. Yet both reflect equally the poet's keenly observant eye and deeply felt love of nature.

In his preface to Wordsworth's poems he concluded:

As Wordsworth reclined in a grove sometime in 1798, it grieved his heart to think 'what man has made of man.' To many in these islands nearly two hundred years later, it may be grievous to think what man has made of nature. It is the editor's hope that a re-reading of this selection may at least re-open our eyes to the price we pay for our so-called progress, and, at best, remind us where we truly belong. For as Coleridge said, 'The medium by which spirits understand each other is the freedom they possess in common' [p. 99].

Thomas's description of the created world assumed a greater vividness and eloquence after his move to Aberdaron at the end of the Llyn peninsula in 1968:

> Grey waters, vast
> as an area of prayer
> that one enters. Daily
> over a period of years
> I have let the eye rest on them.
> Was I waiting for something?
> Nothing
> but that continuous waving
> that is without meaning
> occurred.
> Ah, but a rare bird is
> rare. It is when one is not looking,
> at times one is not there
> that it comes.
> You must wear your eyes out,
> as others their knees.
> I became the hermit
> of the rocks, habited with the wind
> and the mist. There were days,
> so beautiful the emptiness
> it might have filled,
> its absence
> was as its presence; not to be told
> any more, so single my mind
> after its long fast,
> my watching from praying.
> —"Sea-watching," *Laboratories of the Spirit*

St. Hywyn's, the village of Aberdaron and the headland of the Llyn Peninsula stretching toward Bardsey Island. R. S. Thomas often walked the path along the cliffs, birdwatching and sea-watching (painting by Douglas Flewelling, courtesy Scot Gordon).

There are many other poems with this same quality: "The Moon in Lleyn," "Night Sky," "Flowers," "The Bush," and "The Moor." Thomas was never purely a nature poet: his attentiveness to the particulars of creation led inevitably, as in "A Thicket in Lleyn," to thoughts about the eternal, the infinite, the divine. For Thomas contemplating nature, particularly the rugged pre–Cambrian coast from Aberdaron to Pen-y-cil and across the straits to Bardsey Island, becomes a form of prayer, a means of dealing with matters of faith and doubt. In "Moorland" from *Experimenting with an Amen* (1986) he averred:

> It is beautiful and still;
>   the air rarefied
> as the interior of a cathedral
>
> expecting a presence. It is where, also,
>   the harrier occurs,
> materialising from nothing, snow-
> soft, but with claws of fire,
>   quartering the bare earth
> for the prey that escapes it;

> hovering over the incipient
> > scream, here a moment, then
> not here, like my belief in God.

Both in terms of its images and its poetics, "Moorland" illustrates Thomas's artistry. It exhibits the terseness of language that paradoxically is protean in its meaning rather than narrowly precise. Each stanza presents a distinct brushstroke, yet flows into the next because each is bound to the next by the structure of the phrasing. And, the shifts between soft and harsh words and images that yet do not negate one another work like the interaction between faith and doubt.

And recall again the elegant imagery of the eucharistic poem from *The Echoes Return Slow*:

> The breaking of the wave
> outside echoed the breaking
> of the bread in his hands.
>
> The crying of the sea gulls
> was the cry from the Cross:
> Lama Sabachthani. He lifted
>
> the chalice, that crystal in
> which love questioning is love
> blinded with excess of light.

As Allchin points out this comes of Thomas's own immediate experience celebrating the Eucharist at St. Hywyn's, Aberdaron, standing precariously by the sea where the sounds and light of the sea seemed a constant complement to the act of worship. (*God's Presence Makes the World*, p. 149.) The very nature of that experience binds the particular with the universal. That is the quality that virtually all of his "nature poems" possess. They are seldom mere descriptions of the visible; they are also invocations of the ineffable.

What we sense above all in reading his poems is, to borrow from Herbert, "A picture of the many spiritual Conflicts that have past betwixt God and my Soul." But he might not have described it that way. Rather he spoke most often of watching, of waiting, of seeking. And he was always asking. In Thomas's own words "I am a seeker / in time for that which is / beyond time, that is everywhere / and nowhere…" ("Abercuawg," *Frequencies*). Thomas's record of his conflicts lacks Herbert's final coda "before

I could subject mine to the will of Jesus my Master, in whose service I have now found perfect freedom." Instead we have the affirmation, in his last collection *No Truce with the Furies*, that he will persist in his struggle with doubt, anxiety, uncertainty. The opening poem of that collection, "Geriatric," concludes:

> ... I come away
> comforting myself, as I can,
>   that there is another
> garden, all dew and fragrance,
>   and that these are the brambles
> about it we are caught in,
>   a sacrifice prepared
> by a torn god to a love fiercer
>   than we can understand.

3.

Herbert placed his poem "The Flower" in the last quarter of his collection *The Temple*, immediately after "The Crosse," which opens "What is this strange and uncouth thing?" and ends *"Thy will be done."* We then move into the buoyancy of "The Flower."

> How fresh, O Lord, how sweet and clean
> Are thy returns! ev'n as the flowers in spring;
> To which, besides their own demean,
> The late-past frosts tributes of pleasure bring.
>   Grief melts away
>   Like snow in May,
> As if there were no such cold thing.
>
> Who would have thought my shrivel'd heart
> Could have recover'd greennesse? It was gone
>   Quite under ground; as flowers depart
> To see their mother-root, when they have blown;
>   Where they together
>   All the hard weather,
> Dead to the world, keep house unknown.
>
> These are thy wonders, Lord of power,
> Killing and quickening, bringing down to hell

And up to heaven in an houre;
Making a chiming of a passing-bell.
    We say amisse,
    This or that is:
Thy word is all, if we could spell.

O that I once past changing were,
Fast in thy Paradise, where no flower can wither!
    Many a spring I shoot up fair,
Offring at heav'n, growing and groning thither:
    Nor doth my flower
    Want a spring-showre,
My sinnes and I joining together.

But while I grow in a straight line,
Still upwards bent, as if heav'n were mine own,
    Thy anger comes, and I decline:
What frost to that? What pole is not the zone,
    Where all things burn,
    When thou dost turn,
And the least frown of thine is shown?

And now in age I bud again
After so many deaths I live and write;
    I once more smell the dew and rain,
And relish versing: O my onely light,
    It cannot be
    That I am he
On whom thy tempests fell all night.

These are thy wonders, Lord of love,
To make us see we are but flowers that glide:
    Which when we once can finde and prove,
Thou hast a garden for us, where to bide.
    Who would be more,
    Swelling through store,
Forfeit their Paradise by their pride.

Like most of Herbert's poems, "The Flower" has the quality of prayer and thus addresses God/Christ directly. He assumed the possibility of discourse and anticipated that he would receive a response in some form or another. At various points in *The Temple* Herbert invoked the silence, even the absence, of God, experiences alluded to in the recurrent dyings of flowers ("so many deaths"). Indeed "the Flower" follows close upon "The Search" which begins "Whither, O, whither art thou fled, / My Lord, my Love," and the anguished middle stanza (the eighth of fifteen) reads:

> Where is my God? what hidden place
> Conceals thee still?
> What covert dare eclipse thy face?
> Is it thy will?

Herbert differs from Thomas in that, while for Thomas the occasional sense of God's presence seemed fleeting, glancing, almost incidental, for Herbert it had the same sharpness as the experience of His absence. For example, "The Search" concludes,

> When thou dost turn, and wilt be neare;
> What edge so keen,
> What point so piercing can appeare
> To come between?
>
> For as thy absence doth excell
> All distance known:
> So doth thy nearnesse bear the bell,
> Making two one.

Even so, his overall experience was one of dialogue, and a number of his poems have a dialogic form. "The Flower" assumes the simpler form of a prayer of praise, the tone of which is set in the opening lines: "How fresh, O Lord, how sweet and clean/ Are thy returns!" But the sense of an encounter, an exchange, persists. We note a shift between proclamatory praise as in the first stanza as well as the third and seventh which begin "These are thy wonders, Lord of power" and "These are thy wonders, Lord of love" respectively, and a wondering reflection on Herbert's own experience of God's returns as in stanzas two ("Who would have thought my shrivel'd heart / Could have recover'd greennesse?") and six ("And now in age I bud again").

Reading closely we detect an even more intricate and profound dynamic. The first three stanzas set the frame: the opening comparing the comings of God into our lives to the blossoms of spring which make us forget the hardness of winter (ll. 1–7); the second affirming Herbert's own spiritual despair by comparing his "shrivel'd heart" to flowers in the dead of winter (ll. 8–14). But the "Lord of power" can kill or quicken, raise to heaven or cast down to hell, his word is all (ll. 15–21). To this point the poem has flowed from, reiterates, the conclusion of "The Crosse":

> Ah my deare Father, ease my smart!
> These contrarieties crush me: these crosse actions
> Doe winde a rope about, and cut my heart:
> And yet since these thy contradictions
> Are properly a crosse felt by thy Sonne,
> With but foure words, my words, *Thy will be done.*

That said, the argument could end: such a God can restore or not restore as he wills and one can only stand in awe of him.

However, it is at this point in the poem that we encounter Herbert's essential vitality. He began the fourth stanza with an eager yearning toward heaven: "O that I once past changing were, / Fast in thy Paradise, where no flower can wither!" (ll. 22–23). Then he described his actual experience of life, a recurrent pattern of blossoming and withering, of vivifying freshets and sapping droughts, a pattern that gives weight and color to the cry "Who would have thought my shrivel'd heart / Could have recover'd greennesse?" (ll. 8–9). With happy wonder Herbert proclaimed "And now in age I bud again" (l. 36): he continued to live and to write, to savor the dew and rain, to delight in "versing." Above all he recognized his full experience, the ebb and flow of life itself, as a blessing. He returned to praise, now addressed not to the "Lord of power" whose inscrutable judgments we endure as proofs of that power, but to the "Lord of love" who can and does restore us time and again.

It is not power, but love, which makes "us see we are but flowers that glide" (l. 44). Herbert did not deny this world, but accepted it for what it is. Indeed he did more: he celebrated the reality of human life "as we actually live it from moment to moment." Both pleasures and sorrows are integral to that reality and in a sense both are goods. Both become miseries when we make them ends in themselves, when we try to make ourselves more than we are. Strikingly, though not surprisingly, Herbert carried this idea forward in the poem which immediately follows, "Dotage." And what we must remember about both poems is that they follow "The Crosse," Herbert's hymn to "this strange and uncouth thing" which looms as the most powerful symbol of God's love and the most eloquent argument for our saying "Thy will be done." But now we see this submission more clearly as a credo for living, rather than as merely a yearning for the next world.

Looking again at the structure of *The Temple* as a spiral, we may regard the sense of submission here as distinctive from that manifested earlier, even in such a poem as "The Collar." Louis Martz asserts:

> "The Flower" is a poem of summation, of spiritual achievement. From here on, in the remaining twenty-eight poems of the "Church," griefs melt away: they are remembered as traces and twinges of a serious illness, but with a tone of achieved calm and assurance, accepting the limitations of grief, exulting quietly in the assurance of love [*The Poetry of Meditation*, pp. 311–312].

It is at least true that we can see the acceleration of movement, as in the closing bars of a musical composition, toward the resolution of "Love (III)."

4.

Not only did Thomas think well of Herbert's "The Flower," but, whether in intentional or coincidental tribute, he himself composed a poem of that title. It is tempting to think it was intentional because in the collection of which it is a part, *Laboratories of the Spirit*, he included a half dozen other poems with titles identical to Herbert poems. This is not to say that Thomas was imitative, but in his various comments about the craft of poetry (see "A Frame for Poetry" and "The Making of a Poem," Sandra Anstey ed., *R. S. Thomas. Selected Prose*), he emphasized that, while the writing of poetry is an individual creative act, it is not an isolated one. Thomas, the poet, created within a context and within a tradition. Poetic inspiration comes not from blissful ignorance, but from studied observation and considered experience both of the natural world and of the imagined worlds of others. He admired Herbert's keen balancing of sense and sound (the essence of the old bardic tradition) and his argument for Herbert's continued relevance is convincing. Yet, as previously observed, he was not comfortable with Herbert's notion of the possibility and desirability of a "friendship" with God, preferring "dialogue," "encounter," or "confrontation" as descriptors. Even so, Herbert echoes in Thomas in various ways and various places, including in "The Flower":

> I asked for riches.
> You gave me the earth, the sea,
>   the immensity
> of the broad sky. I looked at them

and learned I must withdraw
      to possess them. I gave my eyes
      and my ears, and dwelt
in a soundless darkness
          in the shadow
      of your regard.
          The soul
      grew in me, filling me
with its fragrance.
          Men came
to me from the four
      winds to hear me speak
      of the unseen flower by which
I sat, whose roots were not
in the soil, nor its petals the colour
of the wide sea; that was
      its own species with its own
      sky over it, shot
with the rainbow of your coming and going.

Thomas's poems do not have the quality of prayer. More often than not references to God are in the third person or are by allusion. Even when he addressed God directly, as in this poem, the tone is that of dialogue, even argument, not prayer. At the same time Thomas was more formal, more distant, in his address. Herbert's prayerful attitude, while submissive, carries a sense of greater warmth, of a more personal relationship. Thomas spoke to God as one does in encountering someone whose reputation is known, but with whom there has been no personal acquaintance — or as one met briefly long ago and whom on meeting again one approaches tentatively. The difference is the one Thomas himself described and which he ascribed to the different ages in which they lived.

Like Herbert, however, Thomas saw in nature the evidences of God's creative power. "These are thy wonders": "... the earth, the sea, / the immensity / of the broad sky." We sense a difference here as well, though less one of time than of place: the difference between rural Wiltshire with its cottage gardens, the water meadows between the Avon and the Wylye Rivers, the sweep of the Salisbury plain, and the coast of Wales with the rugged cliffs from Aberdaron to Pen-y-Cil, the swirling currents of Bardsey Sound, and Ynys Enlli (Bardsey Island) looming like a great whale in the mists. As delicate, as fragile, as susceptible as a flower may be in the one environment, its blossoming, its very survival, seems nothing short of miraculous in the other.

The wonder of it informs the ways in which Thomas used the image of the flower in his poem. While Herbert employed the flower as a metaphor for his own life, for the experience of withering and budding again which describes the sorrows and joys of our lives, Thomas employed it doubly. First he equated it with the soul which "Grew in me, filling me / with its fragrance" (ll. 12–13). One might quibble here: does the soul grow? Or did he mean something other than what "soul" implies in the strict theological sense? In any case he did not develop the image. We can note a difference in technique. Both Herbert and Thomas were conscious of the inadequacies of human language, but Herbert elaborated and refined an image or metaphor, trying to work it closer to "the truth which passes all understanding." Thomas shifted the referent or changed the context of the image, using it in another way, as if to surround the ineffable with a circle of metaphors.

Thus he moved from the soul/flower allusion to "the unseen flower by which / I sat,…" (ll.17–18). If one quibbles with the first usage, what can one make of this second one? What is this "unseen flower … whose roots were not / in the soil, nor its petals the colour / of the wide sea; that was / its own species with its own / sky over it, shot / with the rainbow of your coming and going?" (ll. 18–23). Whatever is meant by "soul," the referent cannot be that, for the soul grows within while now he sits beside the flower.

In a later poem, "Flowers" (*Between Here and Now*, 1981) Thomas observed:

> But behind the flower
> is that other flower
> which is ageless, the idea
> of the flower, the one
> we smell when we imagine
> it, that as often
> as it is picked blossoms
> again, that has the perfection
> of all flowers, the purity
> without the fragility.
> — ll. 1–10

The evocation of an ideal flower behind all flowers connects with the "unseen flower" of the earlier poem, but it does not explain it: they are not identical. Again, that was not the way Thomas worked. Each of the images is like a stroke in an impressionist painting, adding color, shading, texture to a picture that always remains suggestive. Thus the "unseen flower" participates in the qualities of this ideal flower, is nourished by its roots in the eternal, yet remains "its own species with its own / sky over it." And that species was...?

Shifting from the flower to the narrator we deduce this "story" line: he asked for riches and received "the earth, the sea, / the immensity / of the sky." But "to possess them" he withdrew: his senses could not bear their fullness, the directness of seeing/hearing them. Not only can we not bear to look in the face of God directly, we cannot behold the power and fullness of his creation without losing our senses. Only "in a soundless darkness / in the shadow" of God's regard could he contemplate them. Thus sheltered, understanding could blossom.

If the poem ended there we would have an exquisite line drawing of a soul's progress and the parallels with Herbert would be obvious, but of course it does not. How can we describe what has been understood (as much as it could be understood) only in "soundless darkness?" Why even try? Because it cannot be avoided; because "Men came / to me from the four / winds to hear me speak...." We here confront directly the vocation of the priest/poet, a confrontation that brings us back to the larger comparison of Herbert and Thomas in their dual roles.

While doubtless manuscripts of Herbert's work circulated during his lifetime, for he had some reputation as a poet, none of his English writings were published before his death. Thus, while making poetry was integral to Herbert's life and the main body of his work manifests the spiritual content of that life, in a sense he became a public poet only posthumously. Thomas published his first book of poems, *The Stones of the Field*, in 1946 and was a publishing poet for over a half-century. His range is far broader and includes nature poems, love poems, and poems about Wales, poems evoked by works of art, as well as "religious" poems. And while he prepared periodic collections of his works, none of them have the studied architecture of *The Temple*.

"Men came / to me from the four / winds to hear me speak ..." not simply because the narrator possesses some bardic knowledge which they seek, but because they desire words of faith, faithful words, however elusive or allusive, about a truth that passes understanding, God's presence in our lives. Faith gives evidence of things unseen: of the earth behind the earth, the sea behind the sea, the sky behind the sky. We cannot grasp it with our senses, only sense it momentarily, a rainbow arcing over our world that vanishes if we pursue it.

In *The Stones of the Field* Thomas wrote:

And God is the weight that bends the bough
Of the young tree gently as spring snow.
His is the lightness of the summer flower
Of the bee's touch, and his the power
That tames the sea and poises like a feather
Or a loose leaf the world. He threads together
The stars for necklace and his glory shows,
Then hides himself within the cloistered rose.
                                        —"Song (II)"

In "The Flower" we have the same quality, though more attenuated, of the presence of God. Thomas was never pantheistic, and indeed moved increasingly toward a conviction that our best intimations of the presence of God come from his absence, of his comings from his goings. But he never reached a point of final denial. "Is absence enough?" he asked in "Cadenza" (*Later Poems*, 1983) and the answer persists "No." However attenuated in his latest collections (*Mass for Hard Times*, 1992, and *No Truce with the Furies*, 1995) the echoes of the song persist, the "unseen flower" still scents the air.

See the black lightning
of its tongue, followed
by the thunder in my veins.
Ah, bright god, so near

to the ground, do you still tempt
me from behind a flower
to put out my glad hand
for the toothsomeness that is anguish?
                                        —"Sonata in X"

5.

Obviously Herbert and Thomas used the idea of a flower in dramatically different ways. Herbert employed it more concretely as a metaphor for his experience, for his life and indeed our lives as created beings. His metaphor assumes the presence, the power and love, of God and he wielded it to describe the quality of life as we live it. For Thomas the metaphor was both less precise and more protean. As such it becomes a means of questioning the assumption of God's presence (though not denying it) and of expressing our inability to articulate a sense of that presence. The difference underscores the distance in time between the two poets.

At least as far back as the early church the belief was commonplace that man could discern divine truth from a study of the created world, the book of nature seemed an extension of the scriptures. By the seventeenth century the two books (scripture and nature) were being separated. Herbert does not learn about the Christian pilgrimage or divine truths from nature, but he readily uses images from nature to illustrate them. Subsequently the romantic poets would come to regard the book of nature as the primary, if not the sole, source of divine truth. Given Thomas's preoccupation with the absence/presence of God as well as his convictions about the limits of human reason, he not surprisingly sees the natural world as a place, not so much of learning divine truths, but of encountering divinity itself.

Whether we regard the natural world merely as a source of image and metaphor or as the arena for sensing the ineffable, encounters with nature remain part of the soul's argument. And both poets were conscious of the full argument: both were fully aware of "contrarieties" and "crosse actions" which defy our understanding, yet sought ways to live with them like "flowers that glide" and both celebrated "the rainbow of ... [God's] coming and going."

XI

*"The Sky-rhyming Child":
The Incarnation*

Again and again the image of the Cross rises over the poetry of Herbert and Thomas, sometimes dominating, sometimes only a disquieting shadow on the periphery. The meaning and power of that image rest not simply in the fact of the Crucifixion itself, but in the Incarnation. In his introduction to *A Choice of George Herbert's Verse* (1967) Thomas declared "The bridge between … [Christianity and poetry] is the Incarnation. If poetry is concerned with the concrete and particular, then Christianity aims at their redemption and consecration. The poet invents the metaphor, and the Christian lives it" (p. 15).

Of the two poets, Thomas referred more frequently to the Incarnation and to the events of the Christmas story. Herbert devoted only one poem to the Nativity. (It is one of the four Herbert poems Thomas included in *The Penguin Book of Religious Verse*.) In marked contrast, Thomas composed no less than twenty-two poems about Christmas and the Incarnation. Perhaps even more surprisingly, he turned to these themes relatively late with the majority of the poems being published after 1986, including eleven that comprise the central section of *Counterpoint* (1990). Inevitably therefore, this particular "conversation" between the poets has more the quality of a monologue.

1.

Herbert's "Christmas" has two parts, or mayhap is actually two poems that he placed together. The first part is a sonnet and is, in form, reminiscent of John Donne's "Riding Westward. Good Friday, 1613."

All after pleasures as I rid one day,
　　My horse and I, bith tir'd, bodie and minde,
　　With full crie of affections, quite astray,
I tooke up in the next inne I could finde.
There when I came, whom found I but my deare,
　　My dearest Lord, expecting till the grief
　　Of pleasures brought me to him, readie there
To be all passengers most sweet relief?
O Thou, whose glorious, yet contracted light,
　　Wrapt in nights mantle, stole into a manger;
　　Since my dark soul and brutish is thy right,
To Man of all beasts be not thou a stranger:
　　Furnish & deck my soul, that thou mayst have
　　A better lodging then a rack or grave.

This is not a poem about the Nativity, but rather uses imagery from that story to dramatize the meaning of the Incarnation: that God became man, "To be all passengers most sweet relief." Whether intentional or not (and it is difficult to believe it was not intentional given the relationship between the two poets), the echo of Donne's poem implies the connection between the nativity of Jesus and the Crucifixion, the means by which "the sweet relief" was achieved. There are other echoes here that are certainly conscious ones. The striking phrase "the grief of pleasures" foreshadows the closing lines of "The Pulley." ("Let him be rich and wearie, that at least, / If goodnesse leade him not, yet wearinesse / May tosse him to my breast.") The address, "O Thou, whose glorious, yet contracted light," harks back to "The Starre," a poem which uses light both to emphasize the shining glory of Jesus and to allude to the star of the Epiphany.

In effect, the second part assumes all the above and is a hymn of praise. It begins:

The shepherds sing; and shall I silent be?
　　My God, no hymne for thee?
My soul's a shepherd too; a flock it feeds
　　Of thoughts, and words, and deeds.

Again it is not about the Nativity, but draws an image from it (the shepherds) to proclaim his intent to use "all my powers / Out-sing the daylight houres." Herbert proceeded beyond that image to reiterate the shining glory of the light Jesus brought into the world, the light that will cast away all darkness and give luminescence to his own words of praise.

There is an obvious reason for the brevity and spareness with which Herbert treated the Nativity and that reason finds expression in an odd little poem that shortly precedes "Christmas."

Mary
Ana {   }gram
Army

How well her name an *Army* doth present,
In whom the *Lord of Hosts* did pitch his tent!

Quite simply, all else assumes the reality of the Incarnation, but the wonder of it is not the event itself, but its meaning which is the redemption the Cross offers man. Herbert's preoccupation was with the Cross and man's readiness to accept that offer.

Another brief, but telling reference occurs in the poem "Coloss. 3. 3.":

One life is wrapt *In* flesh, and tends to earth:
The other winds toward *Him*, whose happie birth
Taught me to live here so, *That* still one eye
Should aim and shoot at that which *Is* on high...

Even here the thrust is toward the Cross, for "the happie birth," while it is the prerequisite of, is only the prelude to, that astonishing act of God's love. The Incarnation is the given that makes the other possible. It is even that which makes poetry — at least Herbert's poetry — possible, for it "Taught ... [him] to live here so" that he would devote himself to the effort to show God's wonder. He saw his vocation to be the offering of praise, the instruction of others, and the rendering of the delight of his art into a sacrifice to God. Yet the real compulsion to this is not the Incarnation itself, but the necessity of responding to the question, "In face of God's own sacrifice, what do we have to offer?"

2.

In a brief essay "The Qualities of Christmas" first published in 1959 and subsequently included in Sandra Anstey, ed., *R. S. Thomas: Selected Prose* (1995), Thomas commented that a "sense of coldness and crispness ... has become the conventional environment of an English Christmas.... The very word Christ has that thin, crisp sound so suggestive of frost and snow and the small sheets of ice that crack and splinter under our feet, even as the Host is broken in the priest's fingers" (p. 44). He also noted the prevalence of country images in the traditions surrounding the celebration, "reminders of the country abroad, that abiding wildness and freshness, where the strange stillness and hush of Christmas Eve can best be appreciated" (p. 45). He ended with these lines from Thomas Hardy's "The Oxen": "I should go with him in the gloom, / Hoping it might be so." Thomas added "But it is so" (p. 46). These qualities provide the basic descriptive matter for the first four poems under consideration here.

> There is a morning;
> Time brings it nearer,
> Brittle with frost
> And starlight. The owls sing
> In the parishes. The people rise
> And walk to the churches'
> Stone lanterns, there to kneel
> And eat the new bread
> Of love, washing it down
> With the sharp taste
> Of blood they will shed.
> —"Christmas," *Not That He Brought Flowers*

In many respects this is a typical Thomas poem: brief with short taut lines, spare description that reminds one of a pen and ink drawing, and an ending with sting. And, for all its brevity and tightness of form, the almost chiseled quality of the language, it has a central ambiguity. The final lines "With the sharp taste / Of blood they will shed" may point to the hypocrisy of those who receive the eucharistic elements, yet remain fundamentally unchanged in their willfullness which literally or figuratively sheds the blood of others. Or perhaps it is not hypocrisy in the strict sense, but only the fact of human nature that, whatever the intentions people may have on this Holy Night, they will fail. And the blood may not be that of others whom they will wrong, but the very blood of Jesus already shed for their redemption, but in a sense bound to be shed again because of their reiterative failures. Whatever specific meanings one might ascribe, the overarching image of the Cross looms above them, for Thomas seldom wrote of the Nativity or the Incarnation without the shadow of that image darkening the page.

"Hill Christmas" (*Laboratories of the Spirit*) makes that connection even more explicit:

They came over the snow to the bread's
purer snow, fumbled it in their huge
hands, put their lips to it
like beasts, stared into the dark chalice
where the wine shone, felt it sharp
on their tongue, shivered as at a sin
remembered, and heard love cry
momentarily in their hearts' manger.

They rose and went back to their poor
holdings, naked in the bleak light
of December. Their horizon contracted
to the one small, stone-riddled field
with its tree, where the weather was nailing
the appalled body that had asked to be born.

Juxtaposing this poem with the earlier one illustrates again an important characteristic of Thomas's work: the provisional nature of each of his
poems. While the individual poems stand very well by themselves, they
gain in resonance when read against earlier and later ones, interacting with
one another to form greater patterns. We approach the individual collections assuming both an interactive and an experimental quality. But it is
as true of the whole canon of his work stretching over a half-century. The
"echoes may return slow," but they return and one's sense and appreciation of a single poem grows by listening for them.

In this second poem Thomas truncated the elegiac description of the
parishioners wending their way to church on Christmas Eve to a partial
line "They came over the snow..." and extended and made more complex
the eucharistic imagery. The wine (the blood) still tastes "sharp," but the
effect is less a rebuke than it is a description of incipient repentance, as the
communicants "... shivered as at a sin / remembered, and heard love cry
/ momentarily in their hearts' manger." And Thomas did not leave them
there, but followed them "... back to their poor / holdings...."

The second stanza weaves the image of the cross into their experience, for in a sense the people themselves, scratching out a living from the
"stone-riddled" hill country, are the ones being crucified. How does the
faint "love cry" that stirred briefly in "their hearts' manger" survive the
harshness of this life? Is it enough to know, dimly and imperfectly, that
the figurative crucifixion which a hardscrabble life in such country imposes
is both less painful than and redeemed by the literal crucifixion to which
Jesus was born?

The two poems may reflect two different moments, two different places, two different groups of people. In "Neb," Thomas told us enough of the differences among the various parishes he served — and his own attitude toward them — to draw that conclusion. Yet Thomas had a way of coming back to the same experience and turning it over to view a different facet of it, to mine new meaning from the same ore — and of conflating separate experiences to give each a new prospect. The new perspective, the new meaning, does not invalidate the earlier one — or at least not necessarily — for each assay extended his effort to surround the truth that passes understanding, so that he might say, not that now he knew, but that he was a little closer to knowing.

This quality lends a particular movement to his work. In the first the title alone informs us that the occasion is Christmas, the Feast of the Nativity. In the second Thomas employed imagery of the Nativity in "hearts' manger." "Epiphany" (*Frequencies*), the third poem, invokes traditional Christmas imagery even more specifically, but uses it more radically:

> Three kings? Not even one
> any more. Royalty
> has gone to ground, its journeyings
> over. Who now will bring
>
> gifts and to what place? In
> the manger there are only the toys
> and the tinsel. The child
> has become a man. Far
>
> off from his cross in the wrong
> season he sits at table
> with us with on his head
> the fool's cap of our paper money.

Both crib and cross are empty. Not because they always were, but because of what we have made of them. We have emptied them by trying to make them conform to our own desires and vanities. For that point to be sharpest we must take as givens the accepted meanings of Incarnation and Crucifixion. As with the two earlier poems Thomas probed the ways of men rather than of God, the difference here being that we cannot assume comfortably that he was talking simply about the rural Welsh. "They" have become "We."

Thomas, however, was not a preacher fulminating against human frailties. He was no Elias Morgan. Again we need to understand the conditional quality of Thomas's work: the title of the collection itself suggests the recurrence of ideas, thoughts, images, the rate of such recurrences, dialing in to differing frequencies. As with *Laboratories of the Spirit* and subsequently with *Experimenting with an Amen* from which the next poem comes, Thomas was clear about the nature of his endeavor. These are not doctrinal poems; they are religious poems—that is, they are attempts to describe metaphorically our experience with realities, including our spiritual experience. And metaphor is always approximate.

With the fourth poem, "Nativity," Thomas shifted from using traditional images of the Christmas event to probe human activity to considering the event itself:

> The moon is born
> and a child is born,
> lying among white clothes
> as the moon among clouds.
>
> They both shine, but
> the light from the one
> is abroad in the universe
> as among broken glass.

The simple elegance of the poem is beguiling. Yet, even if muted, the shadow of the Cross is inferred: the "white clothes" suggest the shroud. Thomas strengthened the inference in *Collected Poems 1945–1990* by changing the order of poems selected from the original collection so that "Nativity" immediately follows one ("Court Order") which invokes the image of Good Friday. Thomas's approach to the meaning of this birth was restrained as well: the reader must assume that "the light ... abroad in the universe" is from the birth of the child and then must ponder the implications of the simile "as among broken glass." The Incarnation is necessary because of our fallen (broken) natures, thus on one level we are made whole again by the sacrifice of Christ. Yet Thomas might also have been alluding to an image that Herbert elegantly invoked in "The Windows." We are all "shards of brittle crazie glasse," yet the light of God still may shine through us. The light does not eliminate our brokenness, but uses it to the glory of God. (And there are also the lines from "The Priest" in *Not That he Brought Flowers*: "Priests have a long way to go. / The people wait for them to come / to them over the broken glass / of their vows....")

Three of the four poems are conventional in their imagery, harkening back to the qualities of Christmas Thomas elucidated in his essay. Even the recurrent shadow of the cross reflects a convention other poets have used, notably T. S. Eliot in "Journey of the Magi." The third poem manipulates and modifies the imagery. That extension of the imagination and the shift in the fourth poem to a focus on the Nativity itself are the preludes to the sustained reflection on the Incarnation in the central section of *Counterpoint*.

Before turning to that remarkable collection, however, we must look at one of the prose/poem pairings of *The Echoes Return Slow*.

Town Christmases, country ones, sea Christmases are all transcended, perhaps, in nativities of the spirit. If one cannot have the lights and festivities of the town, one can celebrate the coming of three waves from afar, who fall down, offering their gifts to what they don't understand.

This is the wrong Christmas
in the right place: mistletoe
water there is no kissing
under, the soused holly

of the wrack, and birds coming
to the bird-table with
no red on their breast. All
night it has snowed

foam on the splintering
beaches, but the dawn-
wind carries it away, load
after load, and look,

the sand at the year's
solstice is young flesh
in a green crib, product
of an immaculate conception.

Here, too, the images are complex and broadly allusive, binding images of the Christmas story with those of the place Thomas then served, St. Hywyn's, Aberdaron, almost teetering on the edge of the sea, the rock cliffs running out from the town toward the end of the Llyn peninsula and the holy island, Bardsey. "The wrong Christmas / in the right place" stresses the tensions between the ancient story and present reality, between the claims of doubt and faith.

3.

Thomas grouped the untitled poems of *Counterpoint* into four sections: "BC" (fifteen poems), "Incarnation" (eleven), "Crucifixion" (five), and "AD." (twenty-two). The cover blurb calls the collection "a visionary work, questioning the givenness of God against a suffering world." More accurately, it represents a sustained effort "to find out what it means to use the word 'God' in the late twentieth century." That effort concludes

> I think that maybe
> I will be a little surer
> of being a little nearer.
> That's all. Eternity
> is in the understanding
> that that little is more than enough.

Within that context Thomas pondered the meaning of the Incarnation.

The eleven poems of the Incarnation section reflect both the search for meaning and the search for a poetic language to express meaning. The conventional Christmas imagery, wintry and rural, which Thomas used in the earlier poems, he here abandoned, or rather transformed by fusing it with imagery drawn from contemporary life. Words like "workshop," "electrons," "crankshaft," and "machine-guns" mix with the manger, the star, the wise men. The title of the collection itself defines the technique. Against the traditional melodic line of the Christmas story, he set modern airs of technology, of skepticism, of "success" and loneliness. The question, both poetically and philosophically — or theologically — is whether from such counterpointing polyphony emerges or only cacophony.

Here in concentrated form we encounter again the central characteristic of Thomas's work already noted: that individual poems which at one level are complete in themselves, at another level are enriched by prior and subsequent poems both within a given collection and across the whole span of his work. Within this particular group of poems he took the dark hard rock of the Incarnation and turned it over and over to see what light technology, nuclear clouds, capitalism and alienation cast upon it — and what light the Incarnation cast upon them. The technique makes it problematic to isolate particular poems, for the whole is greater than the sum of its parts. As noted before, Thomas did not include any pieces from *Counterpoint* in his *Collected Poems, 1945–1990*, nor from *The Echoes Return Slow*. The two are the most distinctly suite-like collections among his publications and therefore the most difficult to excerpt. Even so, we can learn something from looking at particular parts.

The first poem begins:

Were you one of the three
came travelling to the workshop
with your gifts of heart, mind and soul
to the newly born in its cradle?

Was that a halo above it
of molecules and electrons,
with the metal gone hoarse trying
to reiterate: Holy. Holy. Holy?

The first stanza seems conventional with the three wise men bringing gifts to the child, but instead of stable or manger, they come to "the workshop" and instead of gold, frankincense and myrrh they bring "heart, mind and soul." Significantly, the stanza also poses a question rather than merely describing the setting. This is poetry about a question, THE question: who was this child? The second stanza extends both the interrogatory mode and intensifies the language contrapuntal to the traditional imagery. We have molecules, electrons, metal. The poem continues with two more stanzas which are a rebuke to the imagined "You" declaring "You should have returned to your glass / ball, that had other futures...." There follows a long final stanza with a very different rhythm that extends the rebuke, and weaves through it an emerging echo of the crucifixion. Together the two segments set the themes, the language and the poetics for the rest of the section.

The second poem continues the theme of crucifixion, indeed goes beyond it to emphasize the necessary implications for and questions about the Incarnation.

Was there a resurrection?
Did the machine put its hand
in man's side, acknowledging lordship?

There was a third day and
a third year and the sepulchre
filled up with humanity's bones.

Was this where a god died?
Was Nietzsche correct, the smell
of oil, the smell of corruption also?

On the skyline I have seen gantries
with their arms out awkwardly
as love and money trying to be reconciled.

Questions! More questions than answers and what answers there are wrapped in images and metaphors that raise questions. That is the way of it. This is a struggle about meaning when the very instruments we have for understanding, the words that must bear the freight, are imperfect because they are human words. What then does it mean to be a poet, a man of words, when the words themselves are flawed? That, of course, is the reason for metaphor, which is a device for giving words more meaning — but not more clarity. So metaphor must follow metaphor, poem follow poem, to try to narrow the possibilities, surround the meaning. Try again then, try to visualize it:

Top left an angel
hovering. Top right the attendance
of a star. From both
bottom corners devils
look up, relishing
in prospect a divine
meal. How old at the centre
the child's face gazing
into love's too human
face, like one prepared
for it to have its way
and continue smiling?

This seems easier because the form of traditional Nativity scenes is restored even if modified by the devils in the corners. At least the reality of the Nativity is accepted. It is the sequel that is questioned. Who are the devils in the corner? Is this a painting that has never been done or is it the description of every Nativity painting we have seen and treasured? Are the devils there in every one? Among the shepherds perhaps? Or the wise men? Or the beasts of the field? The powerful phrase "love's too human face" challenges us. We celebrate the Incarnation as the great gift of Divine Love, but what do we think of when confronted by that phrase? Selfishness, lust, jealousy? We know the sequel was crucifixion, but was that really the plan? Or was it the consequence of a world already irredeemable? Yet this child — whoever he may be — gazing into the flawed features of love and apparently prepared to let it "have its way" is smiling and knowingly continues to smile.

Two brief poems follow which seem to dwell in the light of that smile, giving rise to hope that we have managed to reconstruct the pieces in the puzzle, the shards of the traditional stained glass Nativity scene, not perfectly — there are some shards missing, some out of place, but closely enough. Then comes the sixth poem, the middle one in the sequence:

BEAUTY (upside down)   SATAN
A G E S   H
 N   L   T
                                                 U
                                                R
                                              T

 The Nativity? No.
 Something has gone wrong.
 There is a hole in the stable
 acid rain drips through
 onto an absence. Beauty
 is hoisted upside down.
 The truth is Pilate not
 lingering for an answer.
 The angels are prostrate
 'beaten into the clay'
 as Yeats thundered. Only
 Satan beams down,
 poisoning with fertilisers
 the place where the child
 lay, harrowing the ground
 for the drumming of the machine-
 gun tears of the rich that are
 seed of the next war.

The harsh realities of modernity splinter the hard-won restoration. A few of the fragments are still there, but scattered now, buried even in the detritus of technology and capitalism and war, the contemporary manifestations of the ancient sins. This is a brutal shift, a turn toward despair, alienation, the human condition in a world where the old truths have lost their hold. The wise man accepts this as a given, understands that the old truths were only myths and that the new truths are... what? True? Myths for our time? Isn't all truth relative and therefore myths are true if they reflect the spirit of the age and the spirit of the age is that all truth is relative? So shape a myth for us.

 Come close. Let me whisper.
 You know — the changeling
 in the manger. Those limbs—

pistons. That smile
that had the polish
of the machine, lubricating
their gifts. They crucified
the wrong one—found wandering
in the country, babbling
of love and truthfulness ...
no down for his bed.
While the other one made
for the town, persuading
the people, filling Calvary
with its derision; knowing
the new travellers in time
would arrive too speedily
to have grown wise on the way.

Do we not have to conclude that the Incarnation and Resurrection are quaint myths for less developed societies? We can continue to use the words if we like because they are such nice words, but let us understand them in the light of the ... well, the Enlightenment, expressive then of the aspirations of humanity. The flowering of human potential is after all the main concern — isn't it? Sweet sibilant sounds that sooth and refresh us in the midst of a life that we know is much more complex and challenging and hurried than at any previous time in history. "The other one" knows we will find it so, knows also that if we ever pause to reflect, to wonder whether this new myth is true, the answer is "It was, but times they are a-changing and now we must move on to the next stage of consciousness." And we will buy that too.

But will we? Clearly Thomas did not. The very tone of this poem makes clear that as difficult as it is to struggle with the hard rock of faith, he was not disposed to toss it in the rock-tumbler of the modern mentality and let the machine smooth out all the rough spots. He continued to turn it in his hand, to think and wonder and ask. In the next brief, striking poem he returned to the wise men: the first arrives on horseback, the second by pillion, and the third by plane to the god-child in the manger. And "The fourth / was a slow dawning because / wisdom must come on foot." He struggled on with new questions and in the last poem of the suite proclaimed:

I have been student of your love
and have not graduated. Setting

my own questions, I bungled
the examination: Where? Why? When?

Knowing there were no answers
you allowed history to invigilate
my desires. Time and again I was
caught with a crib up my sleeve.

The ambiguity of the one uncommon word, "invigilate," confounds the simplicity of the poem. It means to watch, more particularly to watch as over an examination, thus carrying forward the metaphor from the first stanza: history stands as proctor over him and catches him with a crib (the crib/Nativity/Incarnation). In that sense he admitted that he was always falling back on the old story, the old myth. But "invigilate" also means to arouse or make watchful. Thus history made his desires watchful and led him back to the old answer that is never far from him. If that is no definitive answer, it yet was the only one he had.

4.

The uncharacteristically long title poem of *Mass for Hard Times* uses the structure of the mass to express with both passion and irony life in the shadows of doubt. One almost hears this doubting Thomas cry "Lord, I disbelieve, help Thou my belief." Yet perhaps one of the most surprising, qualities of the collection is its wry humor evident in the poem "Nativity":

Christmas Eve! Five
hundred poets waited, pen
poised above paper,
for the poem to arrive,
bells ringing. It was because
the chimney was too small,
because they had ceased
to believe, the poem had passed them
by on its way out
into oblivion, leaving
the doorstep bare
of all but the sky-rhyming
child to whom later
on they would teach prose.

The image of an assembly of expectant poets poised to write is amusing in itself and the comedy broadens when "the poem" passes them by because "the chimney was too small!" They await the poem, the word, but envision it as Santa Claus, not as the Incarnate Word. Their metaphor is too small. Limited by the shallowness of their own expectations they could not understand "the sky-rhyming child" left on the doorstep and so end up teaching him prose! The poem is less about the Nativity or the Incarnation then it is about the failure of the imagination. Yet it is precisely that failure which impoverishes our ability to deal with the questions the answers to which metaphor alone allows us to approach — which are the only questions worth asking. If poetry is mere description then it has no weight, no sonority, and is as prose.

Art fails us as well. In "Mother and Child" from the collection *Frieze*, published the same year in Germany, Thomas wrote:

> A stone lap for a stone
> infant to take his rest upon.
> The word that was made
> flesh has become stone again.
>
> Looking at the future,
> what do the stone faces
> see that can awaken hunger
> to return to the flesh?
>
> There is not time for art.
> Yet art dispenses with
> time by making the casualties
> of it immortal in stone.

If we cannot imagine the word made flesh we can at least see monuments to the moment, but how can they arouse in us a sense of the meaning, for merely seeing is not believing. Perhaps if Pygmalion-like the stones themselves became flesh, but would we not then merely make another monument commemorating the event? Doing so may make it "immortal in stone," but stone is stone and not the living bread that can sustain us. Isn't that what we always do: try to fix, to enshrine, the ineffable in the finite temples of our own words and hands?

Both of these poems return to the problem of what we make of the Christmas events, how we live with them, which characterizes the poems before *Counterpoint*, but now more narrowly: those of us who are "creative"

— poets and artists, including Thomas himself. He often commented, in poetry and prose, about the tasks of being a poet, of employing the creative imagination. Most apt here is the statement from his introduction to *The Penguin Book of Religious Verse* (1963) in which he invoked Coleridge to address the question "What is the common ground between religion and poetry?"

> The nearest we approach to God, he appears to say, is as creative beings. The poet by echoing the primary imagination, recreates. Through his work he forces those who read him to do the same, thus bringing them nearer the primary imagination themselves, and so, in a way, nearer to the actual being of God as displayed in action.... Now the power of the imagination is a unifying power, hence the force of metaphor; and the poet is the supreme manipulator of metaphor.... The world needs the unifying power of the imagination. The two things which give it best are poetry and religion ... [pp. 8–9].

As poet/priest Thomas endeavored to find ways to employ the "unifying power of the imagination" that would speak to us in the conditions of our time, to find new ways to express ancient truths. At times he appeared to despair, or at least to weary, of the task and in these two poems he articulated this not, or not simply, as a failure of traditional religion, but of the creative imagination. Hard times indeed appear to be upon us. Yet, he did not surrender.

In "Christmas Eve" he said:

> Erect capital's arch;
> decorate it with the gilt edge
> of the moon. Pave the way to it
> with cheques and with credit —
> it is still not high enough
> for the child to pass under
> who comes to us this midnight
> invisible as radiation.
> — *No Truce with the Furies*

Another quintessentially Thomas poem: brief tight lines, the words reduced to a minimum, chiseled stones placed each with care, the work of a craftsman. The issue again is not the Incarnation, nor even what we have made of it, but our ability to comprehend it. Like the poets whose metaphors are too small, the artists whose images too inanimate, we have constructed churches— buildings and organizations— with no room to accommodate the very reality we claim to celebrate.

Thomas was mindful that there is a holiness in beauty. While he found this most often in nature, his interest in and appreciation for the products of the creative imagination — painting and music most especially — showed that he was no puritan. As a parish priest his tastes in ecclesiastical art ran to the simple, yet he did concern himself with the proper setting for a worshipping community, though as an aid, not as a necessity. W. Moelwyn Merchant quoted him as saying, "When a farm labourer is docking mangels he has little time for art and I don't blame him — but if he loses his *moral* nature, then he's truly lost" (*R. S. Thomas*, 1979, p. 22).

Still, Thomas chaffed against not the exquisiteness of the arch, but the claims of wealth that merely celebrates itself — or tries to buy itself spiritual advantage, gilt for guilt. That too reflects a loss of moral nature and sharpens the bite of the final line, "invisible as radiation." We not only build what cannot contain the Incarnate, but thereby we render the Incarnate poisonous to us.

The themes here were hardly new to Thomas and one might easily say he was only repeating himself, yet it is important to know that the furies of despair, of weariness, of uncertainty, of mere age did not silence him. He continued to till the "stone-ridden" soil of the land between faith and doubt.

He did so with singular verve and at unusual length (fifteen stanzas, seventy-five lines) in "Incarnations." The first forty-five lines retell the life of Jesus from the womb "until Judas found him" in the garden and betrayed him with a kiss. It is a spare episodic recitation of the Gospel story with the principal emphases on the opposition which his teaching engendered and his withdrawal "into the wilderness / of the spirit. The true fast / was abstention from language."

Embedded in this recounting is the echo of a recurrent theme, the silence of God, and an ironic contrast with Thomas's own seeming inability to remain silent, to abstain from language.

A second specifically Christmas poem in the collection "The Mass of Christ" returns to an idea that he touched in passing in *Counterpoint*. In the ninth poem of the Incarnation suite he describes one looking into the manger "failing / to see the beast for the god." In "The Mass of Christ" he writes as if from the viewpoint of the beasts:

> This day I am with the beasts—
> animal Christmas— staring
> with brute eyes at the mystery
> in the cradle. Emmanuel!
> God with men, but not God

with the creatures. Are we in need
of a saviour, when it is not
out fault?...

Does God even understand or care what it means to be a beast of the field, preyed and preying upon, eating off the ground, lying in the open during winter? Certainly man does not understand or care. Thomas closed:

> ... We live only
> by the perpetual sacrifice
> of our kind, ignorant
> of love, yet innocent of a love
> that has anthropomorphised its creation.

This is not the plaint of an animal rights activist, but of a man who understood and appreciated the wholeness of creation, who recognized that the truly innocent sufferers of the fallen nature of man have been the beasts of the field, the birds of the air, the fish of the deep.

This beast's-eye view of the Nativity accepts for the sake of the argument the traditional images, but uses them to press again the question, what have we made of this story? What meanings do we attach to it? And to assert that, whatever the meanings, they have all been to our own advantage. We have not explored the meaning of it for the fullness of God's creation and so have diminished it. By negation Thomas echoed the view of Herbert who wrote, "To Man of all beasts be not thou a stranger."

We have here, too, a conscious echo of Hardy's "The Oxen," and, perhaps as well, the echo of a tradition in Christian poetry that goes back to the fifth-century poet Prudentius who declared: "Fortunate indeed the beasts, and the masters of the beasts, / Who know how to glorify their Lord together." We have estranged ourselves from God by denying the unity of creation. The price of that denial is the ravaging of the world around us—and the diminution of our moral natures.

5.

Reviewing all these poems we can detect shifts of tone, changes in the use of images, and alterations in perspective, but for all the shifts, changes, and alterations there is a stubborn consistency: a commitment to asking the hard questions. Thomas was a poet of the Cross and the shadow of the Cross we discern over much of his work, yet the sheer number of poems devoted to the Nativity demonstrates his understanding of the indivisibility of the Incarnation and the Crucifixion, that what we make of the Crucifixion depends on what we make of the Incarnation. The central question of Christianity remains "Who do you say that I am?"

Recall again Hardy's lines "I should go with him in the gloom / Hoping it might be so." Herbert had no hesitation responding, "But it is so." For him it was a given. While Thomas gave the same answer without qualification in the 1950s, as he struggled on his pilgrim's way to find meaning for religious language, he hesitated. Yet he, like Herbert, would say "I will go searching, till I finde a sun." His long and persistent effort to give metaphorical substance to what it means, both in terms of belief and behavior, to make the affirmation, "But it is so," seems to end in the brief and eloquent "Blind Noel," one of the final poems in *No Truce with the Furies*.

> Christmas; the themes are exhausted.
> Yet there is always room
> on the heart for another
> snowflake to reveal a pattern.
>
> Love knocks with such frosted fingers.
> I look out. In the shadow
> of so vast a God I shiver, unable
> to detect the child for the whiteness.

There is weariness here, resignation even to the fact that words finally fail us, that the answers we give to the dark, hard questions are imperfect, flawed, partial because words do fail us even if we build metaphors with them, even the well-crafted words of the poet. But there would be no truce, no cessation of his efforts so long as he lived and wrote. In a remembrance of Thomas published as part of a tribute to him after his death in the *New Welsh Review* (No. 51, Winter 2000–2001), Rowan Williams, then Archbishop of Wales and now Archbishop of Canterbury and himself an example of the Anglican tradition of learned clergy, chose to focus on "Blind Noel" as a characteristic example both of Thomas's poetic and the fidelity with which he pursued his task over his whole life.

There is no faith without doubt, but doubt exists only where there is faith. And in that shadowland we must try to live the metaphor.

XII

"This Strange and Uncouth Thing": The Good Friday Poems

In examining various aspects of their works, the ways in which Herbert and Thomas treated ideas and images, we have consistently moved within the shadow of the Cross. It is the sign of God's love, the price of man's sin, the object of the Christian's faith, the great question looming on the horizon of his life. And it is indeed the ubiquitous image in their poetry. To write of it, to write of the ways in which they used it, we would have to range over the whole body of their works. In what follows, I will refer broadly to their poems, but my focus is narrower: to examine the ones each wrote entitled "Good Friday." Such an exercise illustrates by example what they make of the Cross.

1.

As with "Christmas" and "Easter," Herbert's "Good Friday" is a double poem, two distinct parts, each having its own form and perspective, yet written in a common voice to a single theme. In his introduction to *A Choice of George Herbert's Verse*, Thomas stated, "His main theme is love, Christian love; the love that is in God, and the charity that attends a true Christian..." (p. 13). The whole thrust of Herbert's contemplation of the events of Good Friday was to answer the question of how he could determine and describe the magnitude of God's love.

> O, my chief good,
> How shall I measure out thy bloud?
> How shall I count what thee befell
>   And each grief tell?

Shall I thy woes
Number according to thy foes
Or, since one starre show'd thy first breath,
Shall all thy death?

Or shall each leaf,
Which falls in Autumne, score a grief?
Or can not leaves, but fruit, be signe
Of the true vine?

Then let each houre
Of my whole life one grief devoure;
That thy distresse through all may runne,
And be my sunne.

Or rather let
My severall sins their sorrows get;
That as each beast his cure doth knowe,
Each sinne may so.

The blood he would measure, the griefs he would count, the woes he would number, are the degrees of God's love.

The Cross demonstrates God's love, a thought which prompted from Herbert the propitiatory response that, as a sign of his own reciprocal love, each hour of his life would take up one of Christ's griefs, to share the burden as it were. This was a bold and foolishly brave statement which he quickly recognized for what it was. He shifted his ground and instead asked that his sins might pair with a particular moment of Christ's agony, not as compensatory, but that they themselves might be healed.

While lacking the graphic particularity of the Great Litany ("By thine agony and bloody sweat"), Herbert's poem nonetheless evokes the same level of specificity. He means to make clear that God's love is not an ethereal concept, but is real and tangible, as real and tangible as the sufferings Jesus endured on the cross. The cross ("this strange and uncouth thing" as Herbert called it in another poem) is ever with him in his poetry, and here, though it is not mentioned, the cruciform pattern of the stanzas makes it a visual, rather than merely a mental, image. This same logic led him to eschew the various external measures—God's foes, stars, leaves, fruit—and fix the measure in himself, in the hours of his days and in his "severall sins," indeed in his own body. Only thus could he measure or comprehend the God-man's sacrifice, the blood of divine love. This was

The interior of Bemerton St. Andrew's. Herbert is buried either beneath or to the north (left) of the altar. (There is no inscription.)

not an act of supererogation, but rather was the unavoidable consequence of the fact that for Herbert the ultimate source of his poetry was his own lived experience. He could only begin to grasp the immensity of God's love by considering what volume of so precious a balm would be required to heal him.

Having come to some understanding of the measure of God's love, Herbert, in the second part, considered the consequences of it:

> Since bloud is fittest, Lord, to write
> Thy sorrows in, and bloudie fight;
> My heart hath store, write there, where in
> One box doth lie both ink and sinne:
>
> That when sinne spies so many foes,
> Thy whips, thy nails, thy wounds, thy woes,
> All come to lodge there, sinne may say,
> *No room for me*, and fly away.
>
> Sinne being gone, oh fill the place,
> And keep possession with thy grace;
> Lest sinne take courage and return,
> And all thy writings blot or burn.

The heart serves as a dual symbol, for it is in the heart of man that sin takes root, but the heart's blood also recalls the sacrifice of the Cross. He wrote then of the sorrows of Jesus at the crucifixion in this crimson ink, and so thereby the heart becomes filled with God's grace, leaving no room for sin to root and grow. But the final verse makes clear the continuous nature of man's struggle, the possibility of stumbling again, of the weed of sin once more taking root.

The imagery here seems awkward. Pondering it, we wonder whether Herbert was aware of William Harvey's work on the circulation of the blood and whether it informs the imagery. Perhaps that would clarify his usage here. In any case what we have is an apt illustration of Herbert's technique of using double, indeed multiple meanings. Like the other "metaphysical poets," Herbert regularly used puns. One scholar, Heather Asols, has argued that the key to his language is equivocation. (*Equivocal Predication: George Herbert's Way to God.*) Another way of putting it is that, like Thomas, he was always conscious of the limits of human language, the necessity of making successive approximations to approach the mind of God. The technique of these double poems itself illustrates this.

"Good Friday" occurs early in *The Temple*, immediately after "The Sinner" and in a sequence that leads to "Easter" and "Easter Wings." This placement only reiterates what Herbert had already established with the opening poems of the central body of the work "The Church." The first poem is "The Altar," which concludes "O let thy blessed SACRIFICE be mine, / And sanctifie this ALTAR to be thine." (This poem, too, is a visual pun, having the form of an altar.) Thus Christ's sacrifice on the Cross is the baseline from which all else proceeds. Herbert left no doubt of that with the second poem, "Sacrifice." By far the longest poem in "The Church" (252 lines), it is a recitative ascribed to Jesus himself recounting the events of Good Friday. Each stanza ends with the words "Was ever grief like mine?" or occasionally "Never was grief like mine"—refrains that echo in "Good Friday." Throughout we encounter lines affirming the idea of the Atonement:

> Then with a scarlet robe they me aray;
> Which shews my bloud to be the onely way
> And cordiall left to repair mans decay ... [ll. 157–159]
> Man stole the fruit, but I must climbe the tree ... [l. 202]

> In healing not my self, there doth consist
> All that salvation which ye now resist;
> Your safetie in my sicknesse doth subsist ... [ll. 225–227]

> My wo, mans weal: and now I bow my head ... [l. 250]

Though "The Sacrifice" is certainly not the best of Herbert's poems, it is formative, for it is to this voice from the Cross, this story, this grief, that Herbert returned again and again. Against it, all of Herbert's own griefs and perturbations of mind and spirit could be measured and ultimately absorbed — as are those of any Christian's. The poem has a peculiar force in the fact that the poet puts the story in the voice of Jesus. Thus it becomes and always remains in the present tense, always speaking in the here and now to "all ye, who passe by" — including Herbert. And it informs all the subsequent poems, few more directly than "Good Friday."

The anguish of Jesus is not simply the physical pain of crucifixion. The reiterative "Was ever grief like mine?" follows stanzas in which he describes how men, God's own creatures, have turned the gifts of creation against him. And the response of God consistently has been that he has endured it, as Jesus now endures the pain of the Cross.

Like most of Herbert's poems, "Good Friday" has the form of a prayer and thus addresses God/Christ directly. He assumed the possibility of discourse and anticipates that he will receive a response in some form or another. Though at some points in *The Temple*, he suffered the silence, even the absence, of God, his overall experience is one of dialogue. One might even read this poem as the result of such a dialogue. The first three stanzas are a series of interrogatories, prayerful to be sure. The different form of the next two stanzas and of the second part gives the sense that there has been a response: "All right, if that's true 'then let each houre / Of my whole life one grief devoure....'" It has the same sense of surrender that one finds in "The Collar," "Submission," and "Love (III)," all poems which replicate the overall dynamic of Herbert's life and poetry.

Another apt illustration of that dynamic is "The Crosse," which immediately precedes "The Flower" and from the opening line of which I have drawn the title for this essay:

> What is this strange and uncouth thing?
>   To make me sigh, and seek, and faint, and die,
> Untill I had some place, where I might sing,
>   And serve thee; and not onely I,
> But all my wealth and family might combine
> To set thy honour up, as our designe.

The title leads one immediately to think of the Cross of Calvary and the question leads one back to the anguish described in telling detail in "The Sacrifice," to the redeeming act which so moved Herbert that he accepted the call to the priesthood. Then the second stanza inverts the image:

> And then when after much delay,
> Much wrastling, many a combate, this deare end,
> So much desir'd, is giv'n, to take away
>   My power to serve thee; to unbend
> All my abilities, my designes confound,
> And lay my threatnings bleeding on the ground.

Now it is Herbert's cross, the frailties and ill health which bore down on his efforts to fulfill the call. Here and in the third stanza ("I am in all a weak disabled thing") the echoes of the "Affliction" poems return. The fourth and fifth stanzas, however, bring another echo: the recurrent, halting, yet progressively clearer sense that this cross is his own making, the fruit of his desire to set the terms of his service ("Besides, things sort not to my will ... To have my aims.")

The recognition that lurking pride, the understanding finally that even his sense of unworthiness disguised his own willfulness, forces him back toward the center point, the true Cross. In the final stanza the voice shifts again to that of prayer:

> Ah my deare Father, ease my smarte!
> These contrarieties crush me: these crosse actions
> Doe winde a rope, and cut my heart:
>   And yet since these thy contradictions
> Are properly a crosse felt by thy Sonne,
> With but four words, my words, *Thy will be done.*

With the striking pun, "these crosse actions," his gaze returns to the Cross of Calvary and he makes the words of Jesus his own.

The spiral movement of always turning and turning again continues with each rising orbit drawing closer to the center point.

2.

Thomas's "Good Friday" seems a far cry from Herbert's "prayerful art."

> It was quiet. What had the sentry
> to cry, but that it was the ninth hour
> and all was not well? The darkness
> began to lift, but it was not the mind

was illumined. The carpenter
had done his work well to sustain
the carpenter's burden; the Cross an example
of the power of art to transcend timber.

Again a typical Thomas poem: brief, even terse, having the appearance of a minimalist description of events, the force of the final lines driving one back into the poem itself. The sound and sense reflect his understanding of the poet's craft. And it is typical in another way: while it is clearly evocative of the Crucifixion, it works by allusion, rather than by detailed description — and the allusions themselves have multiple meanings.

Consider each of the central sentences: (1) "What had the sentry to cry, but that it was the ninth hour and all was not well?" The first is a rhetorical question implying that no other answer is possible, but the asking implies the alternative response "All is well," even if it is not plausible. The one also asks in what way are things not well? Because the death on the cross ended the expectations of those who followed Jesus? Or because that death loosed something beyond human understanding?

(2) "The darkness began to lift, but it was not the mind / was illumined." This second sentence seems to intensify the sense of unease, for while the physical darkness lifts, no clear answers come. Indeed, what comes instead is the question that will challenge century after century of human beings. What is this truth that passes human understanding? As noted, for Herbert that truth was the love of God, the height and depth and breadth of which is of a magnitude the human mind cannot imagine. For Thomas the truth is a nettle one cannot grasp so firmly. In response to a proclamation that epitomizes what might be called "bumper sticker theology," George Buttrick once remarked that "Christ is not the answer; he is the question." Thomas might say "The Cross is the question." As he writes "The darkness began to lift, but it was not the mind / was illumined."

(3) "The carpenter had done his work well to sustain the carpenter's burden." At first glance this seems the easiest of the three. The art of the carpenter who crafted the cross transformed timber into a symbol of humiliation, suffering and death which people of the Mediterranean world could instantly comprehend. The art of that other carpenter who hung on the cross and died there transfigured it into a symbol of sacrifice and redemption. But how do we understand "the carpenter's burden?" Is it merely the weight of his own body hanging on the Cross? The sense of failure that those words "My God, my God, why hast thou forsaken me?" Or

the "weight of glory," of having done what he had come to do, dying that
we might live? James Boyd White observed of Herbert's "Sacrifice,"

> There is here a partial performance of an answer to the question
> raised above, why Christ must die: it is not Adam's sin, or God's
> implacable justice that requires this, but our own human obduracy,
> or refusal to see or hear or respond.... It also defines a possible
> function for poetry...: to tell the story which, in the nature of things,
> Christ himself cannot tell, that of his own suffering, the story that
> may reach people whom his own words and actions alone cannot
> reach. It is to make the art ... of this kind of poetry, a sacred one
> ["*This Book of Starres*," p. 98].

The art of the poets makes of the cross a metaphor which draws us toward
that truth which is beyond our understanding.

As we have seen, even when Thomas wrote of the Incarnation the
Cross loomed over the manger. In that regard one of the most evocative
of his poems is "The Coming," one of the final poems in his 1972 collection *H'm*. Here the incarnation is entirely subsumed by the redemptive
cross. It describes God and "the son," outside of time regarding the tor-
tured world, "a small globe" held in God's hand. There they saw

> On a bare
> Hill, a bare tree saddened
> The sky. Many people
> Held out their thin arms
> To it, as though waiting
> For a vanished April
> To return to its crossed
> Boughs. The son watched
> Them. Let me go there, he said.
> —ll. 12–20

Like all images that recur in his work, the image of the Cross is protean in its meanings, never fixed, never final. That is vividly evident in the
"Crucifixion" section of *Counterpoint*. The shortest of the four sequences,
it draws together with concentrated force all the probing questions which
have driven his art. In seeming anticipation of White's comment about "a
possible function for poetry," Thomas asserted:

> Today
> there is only this one option
> before me. Remembering,

as one goes out into space,
on the way to the sun,
how dark it will grow,
I stare up into the darkness
of his countenance, knowing it
a reflection of the three days and nights
at the back of love's looking-
glass even a god must spend.

We remember the story, but we remember through the tangle of history, the cacophony of the machines, the silence of God. Racing to the edges of the universe we encounter not illumination, but darkness, not answers, but questions.

Not the empty tomb
but the uninhabited
cross. Look long enough
and you will see the arms
put on leaves. Not a crown
of thorns, but a crown of flowers
haloing it, with a bird singing
as though perched on paradise's threshold.

The question: is "this strange and uncouth thing" the tree of life? And if we say yes, what do we make of it?

We have over-furnished
our faith. Our churches
are as limousines in the procession
towards heaven. But the verities
remain: a de-nuclearised
cross, uncontaminated
by our coinage; the chalice's
ichor; and one crumb of bread
on the tongue for the bird-like
intelligence to be made tame by.

The Cross remains and the gift from the cross: "The simplicity of the Sacrament absolved him from the complexities of the Word." The "echoes return slow."

> Darkness arrived at
> midday, the shadow
> of whose wing? The blood
> ticked from the cross, but it was not
> their time it kept. It was no
> time at all, but the accompaniment
> to a face staring,
> as over twenty centuries
> it has stared, from unfathomable
> darkness into unfathomable light.

John McElhenney reports that in a conversation with Thomas in 1994, the poet said that he disliked the crucifix. Thomas remarked that "The cross is 'mathematical'—if you extend the two pieces of wood toward infinity, in curved space they meet; and the cross as two crossed pieces of wood ... points to something more profound than anything in Buddhism or Taoism." In "The Word," *Mass for Hard Times*, he wrote:

> Some of us run, some loiter;
> some of us turn aside
>
> to erect the Calvary
> that is our signpost, arms
>
> pointing in opposite directions
> to bring us in the end
>
> to the same place, so impossible
> is it to escape love....

Once a reader has encountered the image of the Cross in other Thomas poems, the closing words of "Good Friday" become even more forceful: "The Cross an example / of the power of art to transcend timber."

3.

The image of "the uninhabited cross" evokes the idea of the *Deus absconditus* which is the quintessential theme of Thomas's work, but the dynamic relationship of absence and presence which informs that theme we should not forget. We grasp absence only in relation to presence.

Absence is not a synonym or a code word for nonexistence. It is itself a metaphor for the failure of our imagination to comprehend the divine, the failure of our language to describe ultimate reality. Thomas struggled with doubt, but doubt is not disbelief. It is the essential companion of faith. And questions are the daughters of doubt, the necessary way the doubter struggles toward faith. To say, as I suggest Thomas was saying, that "The Cross is the question" is to pose the issue which is at the very heart of the Christian faith.

We may acknowledge that. We may easily grant that theologians should grapple with it, that poets should as well. But we are uncomfortable with a priest, even a priest/poet like Thomas, who does it. But, to call up Charles Williams again: "My chief objection to the champions of Christianity is that the objections to Christianity do not come from them.... Why should the objections to Christianity be left to outsiders? Let us see them, see where they are, feel them, almost create them; and then we may have the energy that belongs to Christianity" (*The Image of the City*, p. xxi). Who better than a priest/poet, someone who understands the limits and power of language, to tilt at *our* images to God, to test the metaphors we use to encircle Him.

That, of course, is a very different responsibility than George Herbert exercised. Or is it? Thomas observed of Herbert that he "demonstrates ... both the possibility and the desirability of a friendship with God. Friendship is no longer the right way to describe it. The word now is dialogue, encounter, confrontation; but the realities engaged have not altered all that much." Herbert's record of the "many spiritual conflicts which have passed betwixt God and myself" clearly describes moments when he too experienced the silence, even the absence of God — as have all great religious souls. That sense was neither so ominous nor pervasive as with Thomas, but it was no less real. Though it is not an operative element in his "Good Friday," the first three stanzas are as forceful a statement as any Thomas made about the problematic nature of human language in expressing the qualities of God.

Herbert's question was how to measure God's love. To do so he reviewed the metaphors we might use to give some tangibility to that love, but he found them wanting. Poetic language having failed, he turned to the narrower gauge of his own personal experience as if to say the immensity of God's love is indescribable. All that he — or any human being — could grasp is that God's love is more than sufficient to redeem his sins. Inescapably he was forced back to the question of the cross. He did not name it. He did not need to name it, for it is there on the page reiterated five times in the cruciform pattern of his stanzas, an example of the power of art to transform words as well as timber.

They will come to understand
our folk-tale was the machine.
We listened to it in the twilight
of our reason, taking it as the hour

in which truth dawned. They will return
without moving to an innocence
as in advance of their knowledge
as the smile of the Christ child was of its cross.
                    Thomas, "AD.," *Counterpoint*

For Herbert the story of the Cross was true, that Jesus the Son of God, died there for man's sins. The question is whether the individual can accept the consequences of that death, can by whatever means say "Thy will be done." For Thomas the question remained the Cross itself. Yet, if he was uneasy with the story, he was no less uneasy with the trivialization of it in our own times, the ready de-mythologizing, the rationalistic posturings, the peculiar assumption that somehow the discoveries of the vastness of the universe have diminished God. Perhaps, perhaps after all, the Cross must not mean, but simply be.

XIII

"To Run, Rise, Rest with Thee": Easter

If the Cross is the question what does one make of the Resurrection? Not surprisingly, given what I have said so far, Herbert made more of it than Thomas: you can't get to the Resurrection without first going through the Crucifixion and the Tomb. But even Herbert made less of it than one might expect because it was Christ crucified which was at the heart of his faith. In "The Church Militant," the long poem (279 lines) which forms the last section of *The Temple*, Herbert provided what amounts to a capsule summary of the history of the Church. He described its beginnings thusly: "… Now with the crosse, as with a staffe, alone, / Religion, like a pilgrime, westward bent, / Knocking at all doores, ever as she went" (ll. 29–30). However, he did include two poems, "Easter" and "Easter-wings" in "The Church." Thomas, in contrast to his numerous poems about or using images from the Nativity, had only one poem referring explicitly to Easter and made few specific allusions to the Resurrection.

1.

Like his "Christmas" and "Good Friday," Herbert's "Easter" has two parts, almost two poems in one. They can be read with profit separately, but he chose to place them together under a single title, and in that arrangement they enrich one another. "Easter" (followed immediately by "Easter-wings") comes in a sequence that includes "Good Friday," "Redemption," "Sepulchre." In effect, Herbert reached the Resurrection by passing through the Crucifixion and the Tomb.

The first three stanzas sound like an Easter anthem:

Rise heart, thy Lord is risen. Sing his praise
                                   Without delayes,
Who takes thee by the hand, that thou likewise
                                   With him mayst rise:
That, as his death calcined thee to dust,
His life may make thee gold, and much more, just.

Awake, my lute, and struggle for thy part
                                   With all thy art.
The crosse taught all wood to resound his name,
                                   Who bore the same.
His stretched sinews taught all strings, what key
Is best to celebrate this most high day.

Consort both heart and lute, and twist a song
                                   Pleasant and long:
Or, since all musick is but three parts vied
                                   And multiplied,
O let thy blessed Spirit bear a part,
And make up our defects with his sweet art.

But it is an anthem directed not to God or the Risen Christ, but to the poet's own heart, a call to praise, more then, a bidding prayer. And the argument to the heart (recall the second part of "Good Friday"), and to the lute — a metaphor for the poet's art perhaps— is the Crucifixion. It is the Cross and the "stretched sinews" of the dying Christ which teach us why we should celebrate Easter. The line "The crosse taught all wood to resound his name" brings to mind the concluding line from Thomas's "Good Friday," "The Cross an example / of the power of art to transform timber." On the other hand, the third stanza seems to look forward from Easter to Pentecost with its closing invocation of "thy blessed Spirit." The lead-in to that invocation intensifies the sense: "… since all musick is but three parts vied / And multiplied." Polyphony in three parts: the Trinity.

In addition to Christmas, Good Friday, Easter and Whitsunday (Pentecost), Herbert also composed a poem on Trinity Sunday, which interestingly comes after a series of poems about church architecture and appointments. (There is a second Trinity Sunday poem in the Williams manuscript.) Given the structure of the first part of "Easter," "Trinitie Sunday" is worth remarking.

Lord, who hast form'd me out of mud,
    And hast redeem'd me through thy bloud,
    And sanctifi'd me to do good;

Purge all my sinnes done heretofore:
    For I confesse my heavie score,
    And I will strive to sinne no more,

Enrich my heart, mouth, hands in me,
    With faith, with hope, with charitie;
    That I maye runne, rise rest with thee.

"...Since all musick is but three parts vied / And multiplied." The intricate play of three parts, not merely repeated, but varied and multiplied, give this hymn both an elegance and a force that goes beyond the simply visual effect of three stanzas of three lines. It is a musical effect, an art that is finally brought to a resolution, yet also evokes the mystery of God's dealings with humanity, an echo that lingers in the mind's ear.

The music of "Easter" is less intricate, but the two parts still play upon one another in striking ways. The complexity of the first part, its polyphony of meanings in a sense, is in the second part diminished to a simpler music, a song:

I got me flowers to straw the way;
I got me boughs of many a tree:
But thou wast up by break of day,
And brought'st thy sweets along with thee.

The Sunne arising in the East,
Though he give light, & th' East perfume;
If they should offer to contest
With thy arising, they presume.

Can there be any day but this,
Though many sunnes to shine endeavour?
We count three hundred, but we misse:
There is but one, and that one ever.

Unlike the first part, the second focuses on the Resurrection ("The Sunne arising in the East"), both joyfully proclaiming it, yet acknowledging the insufficiency of the poet's efforts to celebrate the event. The flowers and boughs he gathers to honor the triumphant return, the sun which daily arises on a world so gifted, pale before the brilliance of the Risen Lord. This insufficiency, of course, is consistent with Herbert's reiterated expression of unworthiness, but it also restates the tension between the vocation of the poet and his recognition that his words and sentences, all his metaphors, can only approximate but never attain the glory they are meant to express. Perhaps then, a simple song is best.

Yet again, perhaps not. Perhaps for all the inadequacies of our language we must stretch the limits of it. It is a gift like the gift of reason which we must use as best we can, though always confessing, it is not enough. And so Herbert moved from this simple song to "Easter-wings."

> Lord, who createdst man in wealth and store,
>   Though foolishly he lost the same,
>   Decaying more and more,
>   Till he became
>   Most poore:
>   With thee
>   O let me rise
>   As larks, harmoniously,
>   And sing this day thy victories:
> Then shall the fall further the flight in me.
>
> My tender age in sorrow did beginne:
>   And still with sicknesses and shame
>   Thou didst so punish sinne,
>   That I became
>   Most thinne,
>   With thee
>   Let me combine
>   And feel this day thy victorie:
>   For, if I imp my wing on thine,
> Affliction shall advance the flight in me.

This is another of Herbert's unmistakably visual poems and, for that reason, is often regarded as being artificial. It may stretch the limit, but Herbert — and Thomas, too — was consistently conscious of the arrangement of lines. As Thomas asserted in "Words and the Poet" and strove to practice in his own art, poetry is both sound and sense. Paradoxically, of course, most often we read poetry rather than hear it. We should read it aloud, but conditions do not always permit that. Whether we read it aloud or not, we must try to apprehend its sound to fully appreciate it. George MacDonald observed:

> The music of a poem is its meaning in sound as distinguished from word — its meaning in solution, as it were, uncrystalized by articulation. The music goes before the fuller revelation preparing its way. The sound of a verse is the harbinger of the truth contained therein.... Herein Herbert excels [*England's Antiphon*, p. 266].

In 1999 Thomas recorded 145 of his poems for Sain, a Welsh recording company. Not all poets read their own verse well, but the resulting three CDs demonstrate that Thomas, too, excelled in wedding sound and sense. We are not here talking about dramatic reading (Thomas commented critically of such misreading of poetry), but about allowing the sounds of the words themselves and of the structure to be heard.

One of the ways that the poet has of shaping the sound is the arrangement of words and lines on the page. That is, the visual assists us to sound the poetry. Of course, "Easter-wings" goes beyond that: it is a visual image, a pun really, of the title. But Herbert's artfulness here is of a higher order. The pattern of each stanza not only delineates wings, through the downward movement toward the center, then the upward movement toward the end it also expresses the motion of the wings.

Herbert described that effect in his poem "Church-musick" when he writes "Now I in you without a bodie move, / Rising and falling with your wings." More importantly, that effect, that motion, that sound, emphasizes the sense of the lines. In the first stanza, we move from the opening invocation, "Lord, who createdst man in wealth and store...," downward "Till he became / Most poore," then "With thee," to the proclamation "Then shall the fall further the flight in me." A similar dynamic occurs in the second stanza. Musically a diminuendo followed by a crescendo.

Obviously, the pattern also replicates the dynamic of Herbert's manuscript, the falling away as he felt weighed down by his weakness and frailties, then the rising up as he recalled the constancy of God's grace. That recollection allowed him to "sing this day thy victories," to feel "this day thy victories." And "There is but one [day], and that one ever." All the grace that will ever be necessary was announced once for all through the triumph of Easter, so that now we may "runne, rise, rest with thee."

Even with this assertion of the Easter faith, however, Herbert returned relentlessly to that other day, to Good Friday and the Cross. That is the redemptive event. There is no triumph over death without death and that triumph is only part of the consequence of that death. What Herbert finds so overwhelming is not the promise of everlasting life, but the assurance of the vastness of God's love and of the forgiveness of his sins.

2.

If Herbert's consideration of Easter turned back to the Good Friday, Thomas's attention hardly strayed from the Cross. We find only one poem among his many which could be called an Easter poem ("Aftermath") and few are the images and allusions he draws from that day. In *Frequencies* we find such an image in "The Answer."

> Not darkness but twilight
> in which even the best
> of minds must make its way
> now. And slowly the questions
> occur, vague but formidable
> for all that. We pass our hands
> over their surface like blind
> men, feeling for the mechanism
> that will swing them aside. They
> yield, but only to re-form
> as new problems; and one
> does not even do that
> but towers immovable
> before us.
>   Is there no way
> other than thought of answering
> its challenge? There is an anticipation
> of it to the point of
> dying. There have been times
> when, after long on my knees
> in a cold chancel, a stone has rolled
> from my mind, and I have looked
> in and seen the old questions lie
> folded and in a place
> by themselves, like the piled
> graveclothes of love's risen body.

The reference to the Resurrection is explicit and emphatic enough that it seems an affirmation of the event, but the poem is about questions, not certainties. "There have been times" when the questions have been set aside. But these were some of the times that the questions yielded, only to re-form. Yet, "one / does not even do that / but towers immovable / before us." We must assume that the one is the Cross and before one can proceed to the Resurrection definitively that one too must be folded away.

In a sense they are not separate questions at all. Scattered throughout Thomas's poetry are references to April, perhaps natural enough in a nature poet who will talk about the seasons of the year. April is the time of new life in the natural world, but it is also most often in the Christian calendar the month of Good Friday and Easter, and with Thomas the references frequently imply more than anticipation of the flowers that will bloom in May.

> ... In April
> when light quickens and clouds
> thin, boneless presences
> flit through my room.
>
> Will they inherit me
> one day? What certainties
> have I to hand on
> like the punctuality
>
> with which, at the moon's
> rising, the bay breaks
> into a smile as though meaning
> were not the difficulty at all?
>   "Sarn Rhiw," *Experimenting with an Amen*

April is not "the cruelest month" necessarily, but it is the time when we ponder anew the meaning of ancient events—and therefore it is the most challenging.

In *Counterpoint* Thomas posed the question directly: "Was there a resurrection?" The only answer he gave was "There was a third day / and a third year and the sepulchre / filled up with humanity's bones." Both question and answer (such as it is) occur in the "Incarnation" section. In the "Crucifixion" section he declares only "Not the empty tomb / but the unihabited / cross." In the long concluding section ("AD.") we find glimmers of the Cross, no allusions to Resurrection. Most of all it is driven by the struggle to hear whispers of the Divine in the cacophony of the twentieth century.

The question recurs by inference in the "Sanctus" from the title poem of *Mass for Hard Times*: "Blessed be the far side of the Cross and the back / of the mirror that they are concealed from us." And again in "The Mass of Christ" from *No Truce with the Furies*: "Does God die / and still live?" In that same collection we find "Resurrections," a poem quoted before in which Thomas described the distance between ourselves and the likes of Herbert and Donne and Hopkins.

> What
> happened? Suddenly he was
> gone, leaving love guttering
> in his withdrawal. And scenting
> disaster, as flies are attracted
> to a carcase, far down
> in the subconscious the ghouls
> and the demons we thought
> we had buried forever resurrected.

The niggling worm of certitude, fed by the claims we have made for human reason and the assumption we have come of age, rises up again. If we cannot taste or touch or feel we cannot know for certain, and what we do not know for certain, we deny. What is most alive to us are our doubts, our confusions, our questions. What else do we have left?

In 1997 Celandine Press published his *Six Poems*. There is here no striking title that evokes an overarching theme; one can hardly call it a collection, just six poems that seem like final thoughts, yet without oracular intent. Their tendrils reach far back into the rich earth of his works, but they are not retrospective. They do not resolve all the questions, yet they present a fitter coda then the quirky final poem of *No Truce with the Furies*, "Anybody's Alphabet." And one of the six is "Aftermath."

> Easter. The grave-clothes of winter
> are still here, but the sepulchre
> is empty. A messenger
> from the tomb tells us
> how a stone has been rolled
> from the mind and a tree lightens
> the darkness with its blossom.
>
> There are travellers upon the roads
> who have heard music blown
> from a bare bough and a child

tells us how the accident
of last year, a machine stranded
beside the way for lack of
petrol, is covered with flowers.

Thomas does not begin with "Rise heart; thy Lord is risen," but with the direct "Easter." Yet, of course, that word carries with it all the weight of Herbert's ebullient evocation — and all the attendant doubts. Here it is the empty tomb that is the question. Or is it? How do we read the message brought to us from the tomb? What is this stone that has closed the mind? What is this tree? Inevitably we are drawn back to the Cross, to what that death meant, to whom that dying man was. And just as we are comfortable with that meaning, Thomas shifts ground. We hear these other reports: of music, of flowers covering an abandoned machine. What can we make of these images? What have they to do with the Cross?

Throughout Thomas's poetry we encounter a solitary figure waiting patiently to hear some word, some sound, kneeling in prayer to a God who answers with silence, watching for a rare bird to dart from a thicket or to waft omen-like on the far horizon. Is there here, however, an admission that most often we rely not on individual epiphanies, but on messages carried by others that keep us in hope, that resonate with other reports, stories, images, shaping our lives and beliefs? Is the stranded machine a metaphor for the failure of modern science and technology, a failure not only to create the imagined paradise on earth, but to replace the flower of some pre-Enlightenment truth. Is the stone "rolled from the mind" the oppressive belief in the assumptions of the Enlightenment? Are we free again to struggle to respond to the question "Who do you say that I am?"

3.

Undeniably Herbert believed in the Resurrection of Jesus, but his concern was not with the idea of eternal life. Rather Herbert struggled with his sense of unworthiness (of man's unworthiness) and with understanding the reality of God's infinite love. The overwhelming proof of that love lies not in the Resurrection, but in the Crucifixion. Thus even in welcoming the happy morning of Easter, Herbert thought of the Cross.

The last of Thomas's *Six Poems* is "How?" which I quoted from earlier, but bears repeating here:

How shall we sing the Lord's song
in the land of the electron,
of the micro-chip? Are these also
ingredients of a divinity
we have been educated to misunderstand?
Our dependence on him is anticipated
by our expertise. Since our prayers
are material, we let the computer
say our Amens for us. We enter
our banks as we would a cathedral,
listening to the yen singing
and the other currencies accompanying
it in Esperanto. In a universe
that is expanding our theologies
have contracted. We reduce
the God-man to the human, the human
to the machine, watching it demolish
forests faster than we can grow even
one tree of faith for our Saviour
                    to come down from.

In a sense these were his last words for us: that for us there is no Resurrection, not necessarily because it did not happen, but because, trapped
by the myths of our own times, we can no longer imagine it.

XIV

At the End

A number of years ago the rector of the Episcopal parish in Washington, Pennsylvania, where I then lived, asked me to preach as part of a series of Wednesday evening Lenten services. The church, a mid-nineteenth-century building modeled on an English country church, had a marvelous set of stained glass windows which featured not only biblical figures, but also significant persons from church history including such Anglican notables as George Herbert. I relished the possibility of having visual aids for the sermon and planned to begin by reciting his poem "The Windows," one of my favorites.

> Lord, how can man preach thy eternall word?
>> He is a brittle crazie glass:
> Yet in thy temple thou dost him afford
>> This glorious and transcendent place,
>> To be a window, through thy grace.
>
> But when thou dost anneal in glasse thy storie,
>> Making thy life to shine within
> The holy Preachers; then the light and glorie
>> More rev'rend grows, & more doth win:
>> Which else shows watrish, bleak, & thin.
>
> Doctrine and life, colours and light, in one
>> When they combine and mingle, bring
> A strong regard and aw: but speech alone
>> Doth vanish like a flaring thing,
>> And in the eare, not conscience ring.

What I had forgotten until I stood in the pulpit and prepared to preach

203

The Herbert window in Bemerton St. Andrew's.

was that at night those within the church could not see the colors and detail of the stained glass. While that took something away from my remarks, it illustrated one of Herbert's essential points: just as stained glass cannot "tell its story" unless light shines through it, only if the light of Christ shows through man can the "brittle crazie glasse" of which he is made make manifest His glory and His word. Without that light what man shows is only "watrish, bleak, & thin" like the washed-out windows which confronted me that night.

This affirmation, of course, was part of Herbert's own struggle with his calling, his sense of unworthiness that held him back. It is also the critical lesson for all who would lead the Christian life. "The Windows" is the last in a sequence of poems early in *The Temple* about church architecture and appointments. In all of them Herbert used the concreteness of the elements to remark on the sense of spiritual inadequacy. The call to perfection (e.g. Matthew 5:48) was a challenge that seemed beyond him as he declared in "The Priesthood."

> But thou art fire, sacred and hallow'd fire;
> And I but earth and clay: should I presume
> To wear thy habit, the severe attire
> My slender compositions might consume.
> I am both foul and brittle; much unfit
> > To deal in Holy Writ.

In contrast, his use of the window image, while not denying his unworthiness, his imperfections, nor saying they are of no importance, appears to celebrate them. As noted in the earlier discussion of Herbert's sense of calling, he ultimately came to regard the conviction of his own unfitness to serve God as a manifestation of pride garbed as humility. In effect he was saying, "Lord I am not fit to assume fully the dignity and duty of the priesthood, but here's what I can do for you." What he came to understand and what "The Windows" proclaims so eloquently is the great mystery of faith, that God uses man to proclaim His word and truth. It is either God's "dirty little secret" or a part of His great experiment that He chooses to be made manifest through such imperfect beings.

Herbert began from his own spiritual struggle with his sense of calling, but the window image speaks as well to anyone who struggles with matters of the spirit. To put it in the context of the claims of the Christian faith, few, if any, can quite imagine themselves as perfect — and there is good reason for that. Even so, some people can understand, can accept, that with all their faults and frailties they still have the calling to love one another as Christ loved them, and can ever strive to live that calling. And they can recognize that if they do so strive, the light of Christ will shine through them, will transfigure their "brittle crazie glass" into the very pattern of God's love for the world. It is that which Herbert believed and celebrated in "The Windows."

Significantly, while the first two stanzas seem concerned with preaching, the third stanza shifts the ground. Speech alone, words alone, only tickle the ear. When doctrine is evinced in life, then it rings in the conscience of others. How does man preach God's eternal word? By a devout and holy life: "The Country Parson's Library is a holy Life: for besides the blessing that that brings upon it, there being a promise, that if the Kingdome of God be first sought, all other things shall be added, even it selfe is a Sermon" (*The Country Parson*, p. 278). But the holy life is not a life of perfection lived in solitude: it is a life of striving, of falling and of rising again, a pilgrim way, a long and weary spiral way, but not one lived in isolation from others. Living the faith is not a solo sport.

Herbert's near-contemporary John Milton wrote: "I cannot praise a fugitive and cloistered virtue, unexercised and unbreathed, that never sallies out and sees her adversary, but slinks out of the race, where that immortal garland is to be run for, not without dust and heat." To be perfect is to be not in this world, but it is precisely in this world that people live out their lives and therefore must live their faith. It is in this world that the love of Christ must be manifest through them, a light shining in darkness.

Man as a window through which the light of God shines in the world: that is Herbert's image. At first glance Thomas seems much more literal: a window is something you look through. Most often, the windows he described (and it is a frequent image with him) are not church windows and what one sees through them is the natural world.

> Like a painting it is set before one,
> But less brittle, ageless; these colours
> Are renewed daily with variations
> Of light and distance that no painter
> Achieves or suggests. Then there is movement,
> Change, as slowly the cloud bruises
> Are healed by sunlight, or snow caps
> A black mood; but gold at evening
> To cheer the heart. All through history
> The great brush has not rested,
> Nor the paint dried; yet what eye
> Looking coolly, or, as we now,
> Through the tears' lenses, ever saw
> This work and it was not finished?
> —"The View from the Window," *Poetry for Supper* (1958)

One might suppose that the artist, the wielder of "the great brush," is God the Creator, but the sense of the poem is not about that. Rather, it is about what one sees. And, in particular, it is about the contrast between the reality, the continuous movement and change, and the human tendency to see the moment, to regard it as fixed, finished. No human painter can capture the colors, the light, the distance in their variability because she can reproduce only the moment.

Similarly, in "The Small Window" from the collection *Not That He Brought Flowers* (1968), Thomas observed:

> In Wales there are jewels
> To gather, but with the eye
> Only. A hill lights up
> Suddenly; a field trembles
> With colour and goes out
> In its turn; in one day
> You can witness the extent
> Of the spectrum and grow rich
>
> With looking. Have a care;
> This wealth is for the few
> And chosen. Those who crowd
> A small window dirty it
> With their breathing, though sublime
> And inexhaustible the view.

Here, too, Thomas saw the fullness of beauty in the spectrum of change. Only the eye can behold this; it cannot be captured in a picture, or in a glance. He conceded that a few may see the inexhaustible view, but for most their own breathing on the window obscures it (as in the previous poem seeing through "tears' lenses" obscures it.) And the few who can see are solitaries, those who wait and watch, those "who believe / in the ability of the heart / to migrate, if only momentarily, / between the quotidian and the sublime" ("Bird Watching," *No Truce with the Furies*). Not, then, those for whom life is like riding a tour bus.

In "The Window" from *Experimenting with an Amen* (1986) it is the glass itself which becomes a barrier, but it is not the beauties of creation which are put beyond reach. Rather the window is a shop window through which the poor of the world see the comestibles which the rich alone can afford. This sharp-edged plaint against economic inequities presents a total contrast to Herbert's poem of the same name and underscores an obvious contrast between the two priest-poets already remarked. Herbert's poetry is ultimately more of a piece, each poem another shard of glass in the window that provides his spiritual portrait. Ultimately one might say the same of the larger and more disparate gathering of Thomas's poems, but if so what we have is a broad impressionistic canvas rather than a stained glass window. Or, to retain the window imagery, one can note the observation that Calvin Bedient made in comparing R. S. with Dylan Thomas and Gerard Manley Hopkins: "Restless and raging as all three poets are, rattling the gates of earth and sky, eager for a sacramental communion with the world, Hopkins and Dylan Thomas are yet like stained glass windows and R. S. Thomas like a clear one" (*Eight Contemporary Poets*, London, 1974, p. 53).

The poem also adds an exclamation point to the observation that Thomas invariably used the literal sense of a window as something through which one looks. But it is not always a literal window. In the title poem of his collection *Poetry for Supper* he describes the conversation of "two old poets, / Hunched at their beer in the low haze / Of an inn parlour, while the talk ran / Noisily by them, glib with prose."

> 'Listen, now, verse should be as natural
> As the small tuber that feeds on muck
> And grows slowly from obtuse soil
> To the white flower of immortal beauty.'
>
> 'Natural, hell! What was it Chaucer
> Said once about the long toil
> That goes like blood to the poem's making?
> Leave it to nature and the verse sprawls,
> Limp as bindweed, if it break at all
> Life's iron crust. Man, you must sweat
> And rhyme your guts taut, if you'd build
> Your verse a ladder.'
>   'You speak as though
> No sunlight ever surprised the mind
> Groping on its cloudy path.'
>
> 'Sunlight's a thing that needs a window
> Before it enter a dark room.
> Windows don't happen.'

We have here the contrast between the romantic view of poetry as the result of pure inspiration with the poet simply the medium through which it flows and the view of poetry as craft. As noted earlier Thomas clearly holds the latter view — as does Herbert.

In his essay "R. S. Thomas: Poet for Turn-of-the-Millenium Believers," John McEllhenney has pointed out that the image speaks as well to Thomas's understanding of the spiritual life: "Windows don't happen" applies also to soul-windows. If one does not work at crafting a window through a spiritual discipline of prayer, worship and study, the light of God cannot enter one's life.

No one reading such collections as *Laboratories of the Spirit, Experimenting with an Amen,* or *No Truce with the Furies,* to name but a few, can doubt the aptness of McEllhenney's observation. I have repeatedly noted the tentative quality of Thomas's poems, the fact that each poem, each collection, is an effort to reach a better understanding, a striving, as it were, to move "further up, further in." That quality reflects Thomas's sense of the finiteness of man and the imperfection of language. It also reflects his conviction that in face of the complexities and confusions of these days there must be "no truce with the furies." One must always be working at the window, making sure it is ready, as ready as a human can make it.

Rowan Williams remarked that Thomas's typical imagery

> ... painfully condensed, unexpected ... illustrates vividly why he is practically the only religious poet of the late twentieth century writing in English who retains some moral and imaginative credibility. In a world increasingly denuded of recognisable signals of meaning, increasingly dominated by what he so often (almost too often) calls 'the machine', the one place where authentic religious reflection can come in is as consolation (including explanation).... So real grace in such a context 'comes in' through images of chill, of cruelty, of absence and frustration. Grace is necessarily what unsettles the pieties of the mechanical and gratification-oriented age [*New Welsh Review*, Winter 2000-2001, p. 6].

In "Neither," a poem Williams specifically referred to, we read:

> You have given us the ability
> to ask the unanswerable question,
> to have glimpses of you
> as you were, only to stand dumb
> at the limits of our articulation.
> Is it our music interprets you
> best, a heart-beat at the very centre
> of your creation? Is it art,
> depicting man's figure as the conductor

> to your lightning? Had I
> the right words, it is the poem
> that would announce you to
> an amazed audience; no longer
> a linguistic wrestling but a signal
> projected at you and returning quick
> with the unpredictabilities at your centre.
>   —*No Truce with the Furies*

We confront again the obvious: that centuries and transforming events separate Herbert and Thomas. But the obvious differences, even distance, also demonstrate the essential characteristic they share: the ability, the passion, to convey "the very quality of life as we actually live it from moment to moment." Both, understanding the limits of language and of human understanding, struggled to fulfill that calling.

Evelyn Underhill observed :

> Even George Herbert's poetry is far better understood by us when we think of that figure prostrate before the altar in the tiny church of Bemerton — symbol of a self-immolation to the purposes of Reality which every artist shares to some degree — while the parishioners waited for the door to be unlocked, and the new rector's induction to begin [*Mixed Pastures*, p. 42].

As if echoing this judgment, Thomas recounted this same anecdote about Herbert in the introduction to his verse. It is an image that seems to resonate.

In his study, *Furious Interiors: Wales, R. S. Thomas and God*, Justin Wintle used as the cover picture a photograph of Thomas leaning on the lower half of the Dutch door of Sarn-y-Rhiw, the cottage where he lived for a number of years after his retirement from the active ministry. My guess is that Wintle chose it because he thought it reflected the curmudgeonly qualities that he regarded as the dominant characteristic of the man, perhaps too of the poet. And if one had reached that conclusion about Thomas I suppose one might see the picture that way. But Wintle never met Thomas and in his book repeatedly whined about the fact that Thomas would not agree to speak with him. I do not know the particulars of the case and so will offer no opinion, but I do know others who were more fortunate in their contacts with the poet.

Thomas was certainly a private person and did not ascribe to the view that one must know a poet's biography to understand his poetry. In any case, I see that photograph rather as an emanation of his poem, "At the End" from *No Truce with the Furies*:

Few possessions: a chair,
a table, a bed
to say my prayers by,
and, gathered from the shore,
the bone-like, crossed sticks
proving that nature
acknowledges the Crucifixion.
All night I am at
a window not too small
to be frame to the stars
that are no further off
than the city lights
I have rejected. By day
the passers-by, who are not
pilgrims, stare through the rain's
bars, seeing me as prisoner
of the one view, I who
have been made free
by the tide's pendulum truth
that the heart that is low now
will be at the full tomorrow.

Bibliography

As indicated at the beginning, my aim has been to let the "poets talk to the poets." For that reason my deepest reading has been in Herbert and Thomas themselves. The standard edition of Herbert's poetry is the oft-cited F. E. Hutchinson, ed., *The Works of George Herbert* (Oxford University Press, Oxford, 1941). For Thomas rather than using the *Collected Poems 1945-1990* (J. M. Dent, London, 1993), I have read his many individual collections as well as various periodicals and anthologies which contain otherwise uncollected poems. In preparing to write I have also read widely in the secondary literature. But, in what follows, I will only mention a selected few of the works I have perused since my purpose is not a review and critique of the scholarship. Rather I will note those works that have been most helpful to me in stimulating the conversation.

I. General

In terms of the context in which Herbert and Thomas lived and wrote, I benefited most from Horton Davies, *Worship and Theology in England* (Princeton University Press, Princeton, 1961-1975), especially volume two, *From Andrewes to Baxter and Fox, 1603-1690* (1975), and volume five, *The Ecumenical Century, 1900-1965* (1965). For Herbert I would add Davies, *Like Angels from a Cloud: The English Metaphysical Preachers, 1588-1645* (The Huntington Library, San Marino, 1986). All represent thorough and painstaking scholarship combined with a broad view of the social and historical conditions and clarity of style.

Obviously I have found cogent the perspective of L. William Countryman, *The Poetic Imagination. An Anglican Spiritual Tradition* (Orbis Books, London, 1999). No less valuable to me for their insights are various works by A. M. Allchin. Particularly I would mention *God's Presence Makes the World. The Celtic Vision through the Centuries in Wales* (Darton, Longman & Todd, Ltd., London, 1997), his chapter on Anglican spirituality in Stephen Sykes, John Booty and Jonathan Knight, *The Study of Anglicanism* (SPCK, London, 1998) — which volume is itself generally very helpful — and *Praise Above All. Discovering the Welsh Tradition* (University of Wales Press, Cardiff, 1991).

For the broader sense of the literary traditions I have consulted the appropriate volumes in the Oxford History of English Literature. Though it deals with the century prior to Herbert's, I have particularly benefited from C. S. Lewis's still

213

invaluable volume in that series, *English Literature in the Sixteenth Century excluding Drama* (Oxford University Press, London, 1954). After all, the sixteenth century provided the intellectual/cultural seedbed in which Herbert grew. Obviously from my references to it, I also admire Charles Williams, *The English Poetic Mind* (Oxford University Press, London, 1932). Another early work which speaks to the characteristics of the Welsh poetic tradition is H. I. Bell, *The Development of Welsh Poetry* (Clarendon Press, London, 1936). He is concerned with Welsh language poetry in particular, yet the tradition has affected Welsh literature in English as well. I still find much to admire in the critical essays of T. S. Eliot collected in such volumes as *On Poetry and Poets* (Farrar, Straus & Giroux, New York, 1957), *The Use of Poetry and the Use of Criticism* (Faber & Faber, London, 1934), *Selected Essays, 1917-1932* (Faber & Faber, London, 1932), and *The Varieties of Metaphysical Poetry* (Faber & Faber, London, 1993). To get a sense of the movements in modern poetry I have consulted David Perkins, *A History of Modern Poetry* (Harvard University Press, Cambridge, Mass., 1977-1987).

II. George Herbert

The web site which maintains a bibliography of works on Herbert has almost eight thousand items. To endeavor to read all of them is obsessive compulsive, if not madness. I can only claim to have consulted an intelligent sampling of the secondary literature.

The best brief overview remains, I think, the introduction to F. E. Hutchinson, *The Works of George Herbert* (Oxford University Press, London, 1941) — along with Eliot's essay on Herbert first published as a pamphlet in the "Writers and Their Work Series," (London, 1962). The best biography is Amy Charles, *A Life of George Herbert* (Copnell University Press, Ithaca, 1977). And as a general introduction to the poetry I would especially recommend Joseph H. Summers, *George Herbert: His Religion and His Art* (Harvard University Press, Cambridge, 1954). Along with Rosamund Tuve, *A Reading of George Herbert* (University of Chicago Press, Chicago, 1952), Summer's work was one of the earliest book-length studies of Herbert as his reputation began to revive in the mid-twentieth century — and it remains eminently readable and persuasive. A later general study of note is Helen Vendler, *The Poetry of George Herbert* (Harvard University Press, Cambridge, Mass., 1975). As noted in the text I also find James Boyd White, *"This Book of Starres": Learning to Read George Herbert* (University of Michigan Press, Ann Arbor, 1994) to possess the same qualities — and his bibliographical essay is very cogent.

Among the more specialized works the ones which I have found most useful are Chana Bloch, *Spelling the Word. George Herbert and the Bible* (University of California Press, Berkeley, 1985); Terry Sherwood, *Herbert's Prayerful Art* (University of Toronto Press, Toronto, 1989); Barbara Harman, *Costly Monuments. Representations of the Self in George Herbert's Poetry* (Harvard University Press, Cambridge, Mass., 1982); and Heather Asols, *Equivocal Predications. George Herbert's Way to God* (University of Toronto Press, Toronto, 1981); Richard Strier, *Love Known. Theology and Experience in George Herbert's Poetry* (University of Chicago Press, Chicago, 1986); Robert Shaw, *The Call of God. The Theme of Vocation in the Poetry of Donne and Herbert* (Cowley Press, Cambridge, Mass., 1981); and Daniel

Doerksen, *Conforming to the Word: Herbert, Donne and the English Church before Laud* (Bucknell University Press, Lewisburg, Pa., 1997). A tough go in terms of the density of the prose, but helpful nonetheless is Elizabeth Clarke, *Theory and Theology in George Herbert's Poetry* (Oxford University Press, Oxford, 1997.)

In the increasing interest in spirituality, Herbert has emerged as a very appealing figure. Helpful in that context is A. M. Allchin's preface and John Wall's introduction to the selection of Herbert's works published as a volume in *The Classics of Western Spirituality* series, (Paulist Press, Mahwah NJ, 1981). Diogenes Allen, *Spiritual Theology. The Theology of Yesterday for Spiritual Help Today* (Cowley Press, Cambridge, Mass., 1997) is a general work, but Allen finds Herbert a particularly attractive resource. Interesting also, but somehow missing the mark, is Philip Sheldrake, *Love Took My Hand. The Spirituality of George Herbert* (Cowley Press, Cambridge, Mass., 2000).

III. R. S. Thomas

The secondary literature on Thomas is more limited and is less readily available in the United States. We may expect it to increase, perhaps significantly in the next decade, and, I would hope, he might receive more attention in this country. There is no biography, although Jason Walford Davies, who translated Thomas's various autobiographical writings into English (*Autobiographies*, Orion Books, London, 1997), is reportedly preparing one. His introduction to the aforementioned volume is a good place to start. Justin Wintle, *Furious Interiors. Wales, R. S. Thomas and God* (HarperCollins, London, 1996) is interesting — and curious, marred by Wintle's pique at Thomas's refusal to speak with him.

A brief, but excellent, general introduction to the poetry is W. Moelwyn Merchant, *R. S. Thomas*, originally published in 1979, then re-issued in 1989 (University of Wales Press, Cardiff). Among the book length studies that deal wholly with Thomas I would note in particular J. P. Ward, *The Poetry of R. S. Thomas* (Poetry Wales Press, Brigend, 1987), Elaine Shepherd, *R. S. Thomas. Conceding the Absence* (St. Martins Press, London, 1996), and D. Z. Phillips, *R. S. Thomas. Poet of the Living God* (MacMillan, London, 1986). Shepherd, in particular, cites Herbert on a number of occasions either in comparison or in contrast.

Over the years numerous articles and reviews have appeared about Thomas, mostly in English and Welsh journals. One that directly speaks to the "connection" between the two poets is Warren Wooden, "A Question of Influence: George Herbert and R. S. Thomas," *The Little Review*, no. 13/14 (1980), pp. 26-29. There are three excellent collections of articles and essays on Thomas: Sandra Anstey, ed., *Critical Writings on R. S. Thomas* (Seren Books, Brigend, 1992); M. Wynn Thomas, ed., *The Page's Drift. R. S. Thomas at Eighty* (Seren Books, Brigend, 1993), and William V. Davis, *Miraculous Simplicity. Essays on R. S. Thomas* (University of Arkansas Press, Fayetteville, AR, 1993). Davis, professor of English at Baylor University, has been the principal advocate in the United States for Thomas's significance.

Essays or commentaries on Thomas have appeared in various broader studies. I would note in particular, Calvin Bedient, *Eight Contemporary Poets* (Oxford University Press, London, 1974), A. E. Dyson, *Yeats, Eliot and Thomas: Riding the Echo* (MacMillan, London, 1981), and the recent Peggy Rosenthal, *The Poets' Jesus*.

Representations at the End of the Millennium (Oxford University Press, New York and London, 2000). Dyson's linking of Thomas with Yeats and Eliot speaks to Thomas's reputation in England. In his introduction he remarks, "Of the three, R. S. Thomas has so far received less than his due acclaim.... I have no doubt at all that he belongs with the other two in stature; and in time will be seen as the outstanding poet, to date, of the second half of this century" (p. xix). In the two decades since Dyson made his observation much good work has been done, yet there is still much more to be done, though for me, far more important than a flood of critical studies would be writings which would broaden significantly the readership of Thomas' poems. It remains true that Thomas is far too little known in the United States.

Since 1995 *The New Welsh Review* has published an annual yearbook of critical writings. Thomas has been a frequent subject. The yearbook also includes a bibliography of books and articles published during the previous year and is therefore a means of keeping abreast of what is being done on Thomas. The R. S. Thomas Study Center at the University of Wales Bangor has established a web site: bangor.ac.uk/rsthomas. Also of interest is the web site maintained by Gwydion Thomas: villagepoet.blogspot.com.

Index

217